Magic Motif Crochet

Magic Motif Crochet

Thirty Modern Modular Crochet Designs

Maggy Ramsay

M. EVANS AND COMPANY, INC.
New York

Photography by Vasile Lupo
Photo styling by Maggy Ramsay
Book design by Jeanne McClow, Maggy Ramsay

Library of Congress Cataloging-in-Publication Data

Ramsay, Maggy.
Magic motif crochet.

Includes index.
1. Crocheting — Patterns.   2. House furnishings.
I. Title.
TT820.R328 1987   746.43'4041   87-5381

ISBN 0-87131-519-X

Published by arrangement with Nelson Doubleday, Inc.

Every effort has been made to ensure the accuracy and clarity of the instructions in this book. Although we cannot be responsible for misinterpretations of instructions or variations caused by an individual's working technique, we would be happy to answer any questions you may have about the instructions. Address inquiries to the author, care of Nelson Doubleday, Inc., 245 Park Avenue, New York, NY 10167.

First Edition

10 9 8 7 6 5 4 3 2 1

All rights reserved. Printed in the United States of America.

To my parents, Jinny and George Dannenbaum,
with love and gratitude for their intelligence,
judgment, humor, and belief in me.

And to Albert T. Cat,
my dear companion for almost nineteen years.
Thanks for the memories.

Acknowledgments

A book is the product of many people. Thanks first to Marion Patton and Barbara Greenman of Doubleday & Company, and to Jeanne McClow of Genie Books, without whom this book would not exist.

I was fortunate to work with Maria Builes, a highly skilled craftswoman whose crochet ability, professional judgment, and understanding of the craft were invaluable.

I am particularly grateful to the yarn companies and their representatives who have generously and courteously supplied the beautiful yarns used in this book.

Vasile Lupo's beautiful photographs greatly enhanced the appearance of the book. I am most grateful for his hard work and excellent eye.

Wayne Marshall, our adorable Karate Kid, brought a delightful spontaneity and sense of fun to his modeling. Thanks both to him and to his mother, Linda Marshall.

Thanks to Bob Reiter for sharing his intelligence, eye for detail, design ideas, and logs.

Special love and thanks to Les and Lisa Reed, who are always there for me and who have helped in every imaginable way.

Contents

Introduction

A crocheted motif is a simple geometric shape—perhaps a square, diamond, or hexagon—designed so that when it is repeated many times, an apparently intricate pattern results. Motif designs can be compared to those created with mosaic tiles or pieces of patchwork. All are complex designs composed of small, simple segments.

We can only speculate about the origin of motif crochet. Perhaps we can thank the sixteenth-century Italian nuns who developed crocheted lace-making; perhaps pieces of crochet were made and joined into a design by someone else, somewhere else, at an earlier time. The history of crochet, like that of many handcrafts, has not been recorded, nor has the work itself been well preserved. Although many remarkable pieces of early motif crochet have survived, much more has been lost. Frontier women, creators of the best-known American contribution to motif design, the granny square, frugally ripped out and reused yarn as they needed it. Turn-of-the-century crocheters, who called motifs "medallions," used them for insertions and trims on linens and undergarments, as well as for bedspreads and tablecloths. The continuous use that such articles received considerably shortened their life-span. Indeed, to some extent, the very practicality of crocheted motifs and their versatility in designs for the home have contributed to our lack of historical examples.

Motif crochet has flourished for generations and today is arguably the most popular of all forms of crochet design. Why are motifs so popular? Perhaps simply because of their size. Individual motifs are small, so that the yarn and hook can be carried anywhere. Motifs can magically appear during lunch hour at the office, in the line at the bank, on the bus or subway, or at the beach. Motifs are particularly useful for large projects. Anyone who has tried to knit or crochet an entire bedspread in one piece, or even two or three sections, will immediately appreciate the advantages of the small, manageable motif. Best of all, these simple, portable shapes, when combined, form intriguingly interesting and lovely designs.

As you explore the projects in this book, I think you'll find the rich variety of motif design possibilities surprising and exciting. That American classic, the granny square, is but one of many square motifs you'll encounter, and squares are but one of several geometric shapes.

Geometric shapes are the building blocks of motif designs, and the initial project chapters, "Squares" and "Other Geometric Shapes," develop shape designs in their simplest crocheted form. Perfect for beginners, the motifs in these projects are worked in single crochet, double crochet, or simple combinations of the two. Each motif is worked in only one color, and designs are created through the interplay of the colors. You will find a number of classic quilt patterns among these projects, including Nine-Patch, Climbing Blocks, and Sunshine-and-Shadow designs. I was delighted to discover how well crocheted motifs could replicate the beauty and complexity of pieced quilts. I hope you'll want to design or adapt a favorite quilt pattern of your own after you see how easily it can be done.

In Chapter IV, stitch patterns and designs transform the basic geometric shapes by introducing texture and color within motifs. I love crochet stitchery. The depth and richness of the textures that crochet can produce are, to me, unequaled in other handicrafts—although I suspect knitters and weavers would strongly disagree. We could agree, I think, that crochet stitchery is worked with astonishing ease. Fancy stitches and patterns in crochet are nothing more than combinations of the basic stitches. One of the marvels of crochet is that craftspeople have been combining and recombining these four or five stitches for hundreds of years and yet entirely new and delightful variations continually appear.

Over the years crochet has developed in particular directions not part of the mainstream. These kinds of crochet, introduced in Chapter V, highlight the great versatility of the craft—each mimics another fiber art. Filet crochet, aptly, was once called picture lace. Tapestry stitch is crochet's way of reproducing color designs and closely resembles both jacquard knitting and cross-stitch needlepoint. In woven crochet, yarn is actually woven in and out of a crocheted mesh. Motif designs provide interesting opportunities to explore each of these distinctive forms of crochet.

Openwork, or lace, crochet is probably the wellspring of motif crochet. Few of us are prepared to work with the unimaginably small hooks and almost invisible thread with which early craftswomen created magnificent lace designs. Nonetheless the beauty of their work can inform our modern designs. The projects in Chapter VI, "Openwork," combine traditional and modern notions of openwork. Airy and elegant designs, they are quick and enjoyable to work.

Before you begin to make projects, spend a few minutes reading Chapter I, "Crochet Stitches and Skills," so that you become familiar with the terms and techniques you'll find in the project instructions. Be sure to read the section "Before You Begin a Project." Use it to determine whether or not a project is right for you and, if it is, how best to proceed with it. Then you'll be ready to get started.

I had a wonderful time designing and crocheting the projects in this book. I hope you'll find motif designs as interesting, involving, and enjoyable as I have.

I

Crochet Stitches and Skills

Abbreviations, Symbols, and Terms

beg	begin, beginning
CC	contrasting color
ch(s)	chain(s)
ch-	(chain dash) refers to chain or space previously made; e.g., ch-1 sp
dc	double crochet
dec	decrease, decreases, decreased, decreasing
hdc	half double crochet
inc	increase, increases, increased, increasing
MC	main color
pat(s)	pattern(s)
rep	repeat
rnd(s)	round(s)
sc	single crochet
sl st	slip stitch
sp(s)	space(s)
st(s)	stitch(es)
TC	trim color
tog	together
tr	triple (or treble) crochet
yo	yarn over
* or **	These symbols indicate that the directions immediately following are to be repeated a given number of times.
( ) or [ ]	Instructions within parentheses or brackets are to be repeated a given number of times.
work even	Work without increasing or decreasing, always keeping pattern as established.

Metric Conversions

Linear Measure:
1 inch = 2.54 centimeters
12 inches = 1 foot = 0.3048 meter
3 feet = 1 yard = 0.9144 meter

Square Measure:
1 square inch = 6.4516 square centimeters
144 square inches = 1 square yard = 0.8361 square meter

To Begin

How to Hold the Hook and Yarn

Make a slip knot and pull it closed loosely around the hook. Hold the hook in your right hand with the flattened part between your thumb and fingers and the bottom of the hook cradled between your fingers and the palm of your hand. Or, if you prefer, hold the hook as you would hold a pencil. The yarn is held in the left hand. Wrap the long end over your index finger, under the next two fingers, and over your little finger. If you prefer, you can wrap the yarn loosely around your little finger. Pressure between the little and ring fingers controls the flow of yarn; the index finger controls the tension between yarn and hook. The piece of crochet is held loosely between the thumb and middle finger of the left hand.

Yarn Over (yo)

A yarn over is not a stitch; rather it is an action, one essential to all crochet stitches. To yarn over, hold the hook and yarn as described above and bring the hook under the yarn and away from yourself. The hook will be between the yarn and the middle finger of your left hand, with the yarn lying across it on top. The hook is then rotated slightly toward you to catch the yarn.

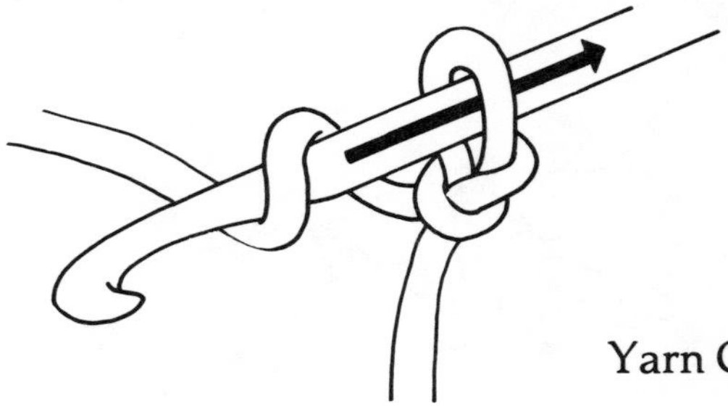

Yarn Over

Foundation Chain (ch)

Make a slip knot and hold it loosely between the thumb and middle finger of your left hand with your hands in a position to crochet. *Yarn over and draw the yarn through the loop on your hook. You

have completed one chain. To make a foundation chain, repeat from *
the number of times specified in the instructions.

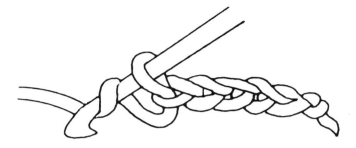

Foundation Chain

Where to Insert the Hook

Stitches are worked into stitches or chains of the previous row. When
working into stitches, always insert your hook under both loops of the
V at the top of the stitch unless the instructions tell you to do otherwise. When working into a foundation chain, it is easier—and acceptable—to work only into the back loop of each chain.

Basic Stitches

Slip Stitch (sl st)

Insert the hook into the appropriate stitch, yarn over, and draw the
yarn through both the stitch and the loop on your hook. One loop
remains on your hook and you have completed one slip stitch.

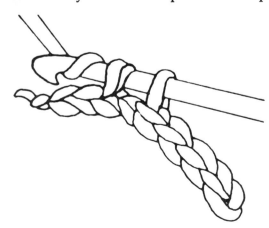

Slip Stitch

Single Crochet (sc)

Insert the hook into the appropriate stitch, yarn over, and draw the yarn through the stitch. There are now two loops on the hook. Yarn over and draw the yarn through both loops on the hook. One loop remains on the hook and you have completed one single crochet.

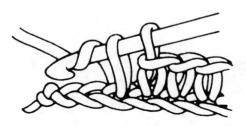

Single Crochet

Half Double Crochet (hdc)

Yarn over, insert the hook into the appropriate stitch, yarn over and draw the yarn through the stitch. There are now three loops on the hook. Yarn over and draw the yarn through all three loops on the hook. One loop remains on the hook and you have completed one half double crochet.

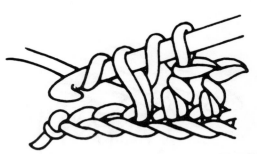

Half Double Crochet

Double Crochet (dc)

Yarn over, insert the hook into the appropriate stitch, yarn over, and draw the yarn through the stitch. There are now three loops on the hook. Yarn over and draw the yarn through the first two loops on the hook. Two loops remain on the hook. Yarn over and draw the yarn through these two loops. One loop remains on the hook and you have completed one double crochet.

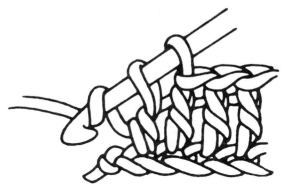

Double Crochet

Treble Crochet (tr)

Yarn over, then yarn over again. Insert the hook into the appropriate stitch, yarn over, and draw the yarn through the stitch. There are now four loops on the hook. Yarn over and draw the yarn through the first two loops on the hook. Three loops remain on the hook. Yarn over and draw the yarn through the first two of these loops. Two loops remain on the hook. Yarn over and draw the yarn through the last two loops. One loop remains on the hook and you have completed one treble crochet.

Treble Crochet

Terms and Techniques

Parts of a Stitch and Stitch Placement

Every crochet stitch has two strands of yarn at the top that form a *V*. This *V* is called the *head* of the stitch. All the basic stitches except the slip stitch have a vertical bar that extends from the head to the stitch below. This is the *post* of the stitch. Unless the instructions state otherwise, new stitches are always worked under both strands (which are called *loops*) of the head. However, since one of the easiest and most interesting ways to create textural design in crochet is to vary the placement of stitches, the instructions will often tell you to work into or around other parts of the stitch.

To Work in One Loop Only

The instructions may tell you to insert the hook under only one loop of the head instead of both. Since the loop used will determine the effect created, it is important that clear terms are used to distinguish one loop from the other. When a piece is worked always in the same direction, as in rounds, one side of the piece (usually considered the front side) is always facing you. In this situation, it makes sense to call the loop closest to you the front loop and the loop farthest away from you the back loop, and the instructions will do so. However, when a piece is worked back and forth so that first one side of the piece and then the other faces you, the terms front and back are less helpful, and the more cumbersome but precise terms "the loop closest to you" and "the loop farthest away from you" will be used. *Note:* When working in joined rounds, always work the slip stitch join through *both* loops of the first stitch or a small hole will appear at the join.

To Work Around the Post (post st)

When you work around the post of a stitch, the head of that stitch is pushed either toward you or away from you. To push the head to the side facing you: Insert the hook from back to front to back around the post of the stitch, yarn over, draw up a loop, and complete the stitch (A). To push the head to the side away from you: Insert the hook from front to back to front around the post of the stitch, yarn over, draw up a loop, and complete the stitch (B). A post stitch can be worked around the post of any basic stitch except the slip stitch, which has no post, and can itself be any basic stitch. The stitch designated in the name (for example, sc post stitch) refers to the new stitch being worked, not the stitch being worked around.

Post Stitch

(A) Pushing head to side facing you

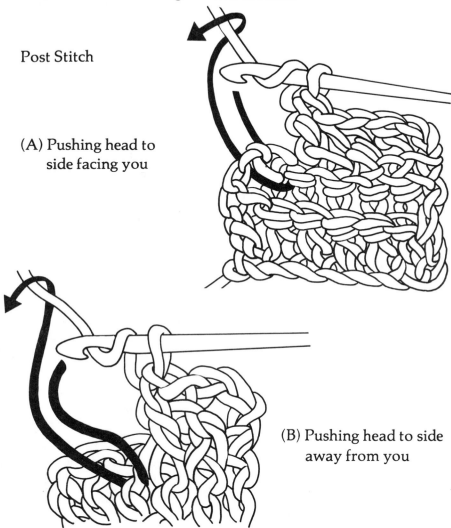

(B) Pushing head to side away from you

To Work over a Stitch into a Stitch One or More Rows Below
The instructions may tell you not to work into the next stitch of the just completed row, but to work *over* that stitch and into a stitch one or more rows below. Since the heads of stitches in lower rows have already been worked in, you must place the stitch in the space under the heads and between the stitches of that row. Be sure to draw up a slightly longer loop than you usually do so that you won't distort the fabric.

To Work Backward (reverse sc)

This stitch variation involves direction rather than placement. Instead of working from right to left, you will work from *left* to *right*. If you are working in rows, do not turn your work when you complete the row prior to the reverse sc row. You must begin on the left-hand edge of the piece. (If you are working in rounds, you will simply go back the way you came.) Ch 1 and then insert the hook from front to back under the head of the last stitch of the previous row (that is, the stitch you have just completed). Draw up a loop to the front of the piece, yarn over, and draw through both loops on hook. You have completed one reverse single crochet. To make the next, insert the hook in the next stitch to the *right*, draw up a loop and complete the stitch as you just did. The stitches will appear to roll over the edge of the piece. To get the best effect, don't work too tightly. This stitch is generally used as a final outer border because new stitches cannot be worked into it.

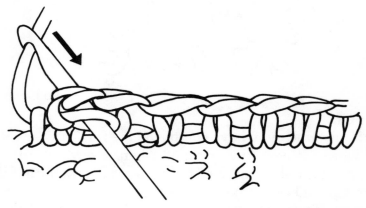

Reverse Single Crochet

To Increase (inc)

Increasing in crochet simply consists of working more than one stitch into one stitch of the previous row. The number of stitches to be worked and the frequency of the increases will be specified in the instructions.

To Decrease (dec)

To work single-crochet decrease (sc dec): Insert hook in stitch, yarn over and draw up a loop, insert hook in next stitch, yarn over and draw up a loop. There are three loops on your hook. Yarn over and draw through all three loops. You have decreased one stitch. To work three-stitch single-crochet decrease (3-st sc dec): Insert hook in stitch, yarn over and draw up a loop, insert hook in next stitch and draw up a loop, insert hook in third stitch and draw up a loop. There are four loops on your hook. Yarn over and draw through all four loops. You have decreased two stitches. To work double-crochet decrease (dc dec): Work the first dc until two loops remain on hook. Insert hook in next stitch, yarn over, draw up a loop, yarn over and draw through first two loops on hook. Three loops remain on your hook. Yarn over and draw through all three loops. You have decreased one stitch.

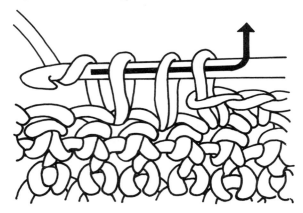

To Decrease

To Fasten Off
Fasten off only when you have completed the final row or round of a piece, or when the next row or round begins elsewhere on the piece. When the piece is to be continued but with a different yarn, follow the instructions given below for changing from one yarn to another at the end of a row. To fasten off: Complete the final stitch of the row or round, and, if you are working in rounds, join the round with a slip stitch. Cut the yarn, leaving a tail of three to four inches. Yarn over with the tail and draw it through the loop on your hook, giving it a slight tug to tighten the closing.

To Change from One Yarn to Another at the End of a Row
Work the final stitch of the row until two loops remain on your hook. Cut the yarn, leaving a three- to four-inch tail. To complete the stitch, yarn over with the new yarn and draw it through the two loops on your hook, leaving a three- to four-inch tail of new yarn. Tie the tails together as close to the side of your piece as you can. You now have a loop of new yarn on your hook and are ready to chain up and begin the next row.

To Change from One Yarn to Another at the End of a Round
Change yarn on the final stitch of the round just as you would at the end of a row. With the new yarn, join the round with a slip stitch. You are now ready to chain up and begin the new round.

To Change and Carry Yarn in Tapestry-Stitch Designs
Tapestry-stitch designs are made by changing the color of the yarn within the row or round. All the tapestry-stitch designs in this book are worked entirely in single crochet, and all are worked in rounds. When you work in rounds, the front of the piece always faces you and this has two advantages for tapestry stitch. It produces clearer designs that more closely resemble jacquard knitting, and it eliminates the biggest dilemma of colorwork in knitting and crocheting—how to deal with the yarn not in use. Working in rounds, the unused yarn is easily carried behind the work.

To change yarns, work the last stitch of one color until two loops remain on your hook. Drop that yarn, pick up the new yarn, and, with it, yarn over and complete the stitch. Give the first yarn a slight tug to tighten the stitch and position it behind the heads of the stitches into which you are about to work. It should be positioned so that when you insert your hook into a stitch, it will be above the hook. As you make stitches, the yarn will be caught and held behind the row, ready to be picked up and used again when needed. Since carried yarn has no give, it is very important that you carry it as loosely as possible or your piece may become distorted.

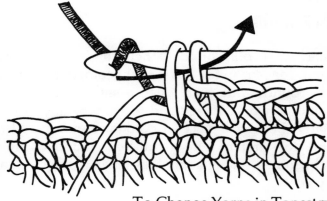

To Change Yarns in Tapestry Stitch

To Attach Yarn
If a row or round ends in one place and the next row or round begins elsewhere, you must first fasten off the old yarn and then attach the new yarn in the appropriate place. Insert the hook into the stitch in

which you are to begin the next row or round. Yarn over and draw a loop of the new yarn through the stitch, leaving a three- to four-inch tail. Holding the tail and the long end of the yarn together, yarn over with both of them and draw them through the loop on your hook. Drop the tail. You are now ready to begin the next row or round.

Filet Crochet

In filet-crochet designs, blocks of solid stitches are combined with blocks of open-mesh stitches so that the contrast between solid and open areas creates the design. Filet crochet is worked in rows from a graph. Each square of the graph represents two stitches, either an *open block* composed of (1 dc in next st, ch 1, skip next st) or a *solid block* of (1 dc in each of next 2 sts). Filet-crochet graphs are read from the bottom up. Odd-numbered rows are read from right to left; even-numbered rows are read from left to right.

To Begin a Row with a Solid Block: Ch 3 (counts as 1 dc), skip first st, 1 dc in next st.

To begin a row with an open block: Ch 4 (counts as 1 dc, ch 1), skip first and second sts.

Every row ends with a double crochet that serves as an anchor for the last block of stitches.

To Work in Rounds

Most motifs are worked in rounds rather than back and forth in rows. To some extent, the reason for this is that geometric shapes often must be worked in rounds. But even when a shape, such as a square or rectangle, could be worked back and forth, working in rounds is the better alternative because a piece worked in rounds has a finished outside edge and does not require a finishing round of single crochet before it can be joined—a big advantage when a design is composed of many small pieces.

To Begin

There are two ways to begin a piece worked in rounds, and the instructions will tell you which to use. In the first, you will make a few chains and then work all the stitches of the first round into the first chain you made. This type of beginning is used when an open circle at the center is not desired, so if you find that the chain you are working into has opened up a bit, pull on the yarn tail below the slip knot to tighten it.

When an open center is desired, you will first make a foundation chain, then insert your hook in the first chain you made, yarn over, and draw a loop through both the chain and the loop on your hook. You have joined the chain with a slip stitch to form a ring. You are ready to chain up and begin the first round. Do not work the first round into the chains, but over them, into the ring.

To Join Chain with Slip Stitch to Make a Ring

To Join a Round

After you have completed the last stitch of a round, insert your hook under the head of the first stitch of the round and draw a loop through that stitch and the loop on your hook. You have joined the round with a slip stitch and are ready to chain up and begin the next round. Do not turn your work over. Unless the instructions tell you otherwise, rounds are worked with one side, usually considered the front, always facing you. When you reach the end of a round, make sure that you do not work into the slip-stitch join, which is the last *V* you see at the end of a round.

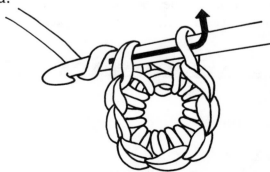

To Join Round with a Slip Stitch

Corner Stitch

Working in rounds requires a regular pattern of increases. The pattern of increases used determines the shape of the piece (see "Basic Geometric Shapes"). Frequently, three stitches are worked into the center stitch of the three-stitch increase of the previous round. This center stitch is the corner stitch.

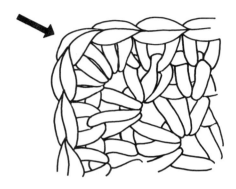

Corner Stitch

Turned Rounds

The instructions may tell you to turn the piece over at the end of a round as though you were working in rows and work the next round with the other side facing you. This means that you will be working around the piece in the opposite direction, so that instead of the slip-stitch join being the last *V* of the round, it is now the first. Make sure that you skip the first *V* of a turned round and begin in the second, which is the first stitch.

Just as the slip-stitch join can be mistaken for the first stitch of a turned round, the last *V* of a turned round is often mistaken for the slip-stitch join, which it normally would be. But the slip-stitch join has already been skipped at the beginning of the round. So, in turned rounds, the last *V* at the end of the round is the last stitch.

Basic Geometric Shapes

Basic Square: Ch 2.
Rnd 1: 4 sc in second ch from hook, join with sl st to first st.
Rnd 2: Ch 1, 3 sc in each sc—12 sts; join with sl st to first st.

Rnd 3: Ch 1, 1 sc in first st, *3 sc in next st, 1 sc in each of next 2 sts. Rep from * 3 times, ending last rep with 1 sc in last st—4 sts each side between corner sts; join with sl st to first st.

Rnd 4: Ch 1, 1 sc in each of first 2 sts, *3 sc in corner st, 1 sc in each of next 4 sts. Rep from * 3 times, ending last rep with 1 sc in each of last 2 sts—6 sts between corner sts; join with sl st to first st. The pattern can be continued in this manner indefinitely. The number of sts on each side will increase by 2 each round.

Partial Squares: When squares are set on the diagonal to produce a diamond effect, an uneven outer edge is created. If the finished piece is to have straight sides, the outer edge must be filled in with partial squares. Partial squares need special attention when they are blocked because the increase pattern causes them to fan out. They are worked not in rounds but back and forth in rows.

Half-square: Ch 2.
Row 1: 3 sc in second ch from hook—3 sc. Ch 1, turn.
Row 2: 2 sc in first st, 3 sc in second st, 2 sc in last st—2 sts between corner sts. Ch 1, turn.
Row 3: 2 sc in first st, 1 sc in each of next 2 sts, 3 sc in corner st, 1 sc in each of next 2 sts, 2 sc in last st—4 sts between corner sts. Ch 1, turn.
Row 4: 2 sc in first st, 1 sc in each of next 4 sts, 3 sc in corner st, 1 sc in each of next 4 sts, 2 sc in last st—6 sts between corner sts. Ch 1, turn. The pattern can be continued in this manner indefinitely. Work the same number of rows as there are rounds in the square you are matching.

Quarter-square: Ch 2.
Row 1: 2 sc in second ch from hook. Ch 1, turn.
Row 2: 2 sc in each st—4 sts. Ch 1, turn.
Row 3: 2 sc in first st, 1 sc in each of next 2 sts, 2 sc in last st—6 sts. Ch 1, turn.
Row 4: 2 sc in first st, 1 sc in each of next 4 sts, 2 sc in last st—8 sts. Ch 1, turn. The pattern can be continued indefinitely in this manner. Work the same number of rows as there are rounds in the square you are matching.

Granny Square: With first color, ch 4, join with sl st to first ch to make a ring.
Rnd 1: Ch 3 (counts as 1 dc), 2 dc in ring, (ch 2, 3 dc in ring) 3 times, ch 2, join with sl st to top of starting ch-3. Fasten off.
Rnd 2: Attach new color in any ch-2 corner. Ch 3 (counts as 1 dc), 2 dc

in ch-2 corner sp, ch 2, 3 dc in same corner, *ch 1, in next ch-2 corner work (3 dc, ch 2, 3 dc). Rep from * twice, join with sl st to top of starting ch-3. Fasten off.

Rnd 3: Attach new color in any ch-2 corner. Ch 3 (counts as 1 dc), 2 dc in ch-2 corner, ch 2, 3 dc in same ch-2 corner, *ch 1, 3 dc in ch-1 sp, ch 1, (3 dc, ch 2, 3 dc) in ch-2 corner. Rep from * twice, ch 1, 3 dc in last ch-1 sp, ch 1, join with sl st to top of starting ch-3. Fasten off.

Rnd 4: Attach new color in any ch-2 corner. Ch 3 (counts as 1 dc), 2 dc in ch-2 corner, ch 2, 3 dc in same corner, *ch 1, (3 dc in ch-1 sp, ch 1) twice, (3 dc, ch 2, 3 dc) in ch-2 corner. Rep from * twice, ch 1, (3 dc in ch-1 sp, ch 1) twice, ch 1, join with sl st to top of starting ch-3. Fasten off.

The pattern can be continued indefinitely. Each round will have one more (3 dc, ch 1) group than the one before.

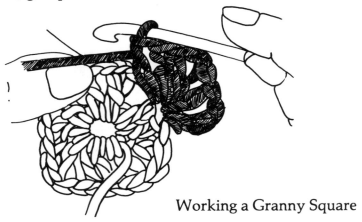

Working a Granny Square

To Begin and End Rounds When Color Does Not Change: Sometimes several rounds, or even the entire granny square, will be worked in the same color. In this case, begin each round in the following way: After you have joined the round with a slip stitch in the top of the starting ch-3, work one slip stitch in each of the next two stitches and one slip stitch into the ch-2 corner space. Then you are ready to chain up to begin the next round.

Granny Half-square: With first color, ch 4 and join with sl st to first ch to make a ring.

Row 1: Ch 5 (counts as 1 dc, ch 2), 3 dc in ring, ch 2, 3 dc in ring, ch 2, 1 dc in ring. Fasten off.

Row 2: Attach new yarn in ch-5 sp. Ch 5, (counts as 1 dc, ch 2), 3 dc in ch-5 sp, ch 1, (3 dc, ch 2, 3 dc) in next ch-2 sp, ch 1, (3 dc, ch 2, 1 dc) in last ch-2 sp. Fasten off.

Row 3: Attach new yarn in ch-5 sp. Ch 5 (counts as 1 dc, ch 2), 3 dc in ch-5 sp, ch 1, (3 dc in ch-1 sp), ch 1, (3 dc, ch 2, 3 dc) in ch-2 corner, ch 1, 3 dc in ch-1 sp, ch 1, (3 dc, ch 2, 1 dc) in last ch-2 sp. Fasten off.

Row 4: Attach yarn in ch-5 sp. Ch 5 (counts as 1 dc, ch 2), 3 dc in ch-5 sp, (ch 1, 3 dc in next ch-1 sp) twice, ch 1, (3 dc, ch 2, 3 dc) in ch-2 corner, (ch 1, 3 dc in next ch-1 sp) twice, ch 1, (3 dc, ch 2, 1 dc) in last ch-2 sp. Fasten off.

The pattern can be continued in this manner indefinitely. Work the same number of rows as there are rounds in the granny square you are matching.

Granny Quarter-square: With first color, ch 4 and join to first ch with sl st to make a ring.

Row 1: Ch 5 (counts as 1 dc, ch 2), 3 dc in ring, ch 2, 1 dc in ring. Fasten off.

Row 2: Attach new yarn in ch-5 sp. Ch 5 (counts as 1 dc, ch 2), 3 dc in ch-5 sp, ch 1, (3 dc, ch 2, 1 dc) in ch-2 sp. Fasten off.

Row 3: Attach new yarn in ch-5 sp. Ch 5, 3 dc in ch-5 sp, ch 1, 3 dc in ch-1 sp, ch 1, (3 dc, ch 2, 1 dc) in ch-2 sp. Fasten off.

The pattern can be continued indefinitely in this manner. Work the same number of rows as there are rounds in the granny square you are matching.

Triangle

Ch 2.

Row 1: 1 sc in second ch from hook. Ch 1, turn.

Row 2: 3 sc in sc—3 sts. Ch 1, turn.

Row 3: Work even—3 sts. Ch 1, turn.

Row 4: 2 sc in first st, 1 sc in next st, 2 sc in last st—5 sts. Ch 1, turn.

Row 5: Work even—5 sts. Ch 1, turn.

Row 6: 2 sc in first st, 1 sc in each st to last st, 2 sc in last st—7 sts. Ch 1, turn.

Continue to alternate even and increase rows until the triangle reaches the desired size. For a narrower triangle, work two even rows between increase rows.

Diamond

Follow the instructions for a triangle until the diamond has reached the desired width, ending with an even row.

Next row: 1 sc dec in first 2 sts, 1 sc in every st to last 2 sts, 1 sc dec in last 2 sts. Ch 1, turn.

Next row: Work even. Ch 1, turn.

Continue in this manner until 3 sts remain. Work a 3-st sc dec in last 3 sts. Fasten off.

Circle

Ch 2.

Rnd 1: 8 sc in second ch from hook—8 sts. Join with sl st to first st.

Rnd 2: Ch 1, 2 sc in every st—16 sts. Join with sl st to first st.

Rnd 3: Ch 1, 2 sc in first st, *1 sc in next st, 2 sc in next st. Rep from * around, 1 sc in last st—24 sts. Join with sl st to first st.

Rnd 4: 2 sc in first st, *1 sc in each of next 2 sts, 2 sc in next st. Rep from * around, 1 sc in each of last 2 sts—32 sts. Join with sl st to first st.

On subsequent rounds, continue to increase in the first stitch of each increase of the previous round. Each round will have 8 stitches more than the previous round.

Rectangle

The proportions of a rectangle worked in rounds are determined by the length of the foundation chain. The difference between the width and length of the rectangle will equal the length of the foundation chain. For example, a 4-inch foundation chain will produce a rectangle 3 by 7 inches, or 16 by 20 inches, or any other size with a 4-inch difference between the width and the length. Make a chain of the desired length.

Rnd 1: 3 sc in second ch from hook, 1 sc in every ch to last ch, 3 sc in last ch. Working in other side of ch, work 1 sc in every ch to first ch. Join with sl st to first sc.

Rnd 2: Ch 1, *3 sc in first st of 3-sc group, 1 sc in next st, 3 sc in next st, 1 sc in every sc to next 3-sc group. Rep from * once. Join with sl st to first sc.

Rnd 3: Ch 1, 1 sc in first st, *3 sc in corner st, 1 sc in every st to next corner st. Rep from * around rectangle. Join with sl st to first sc.

Work as for Rnd 3 until rectangle reaches desired size.

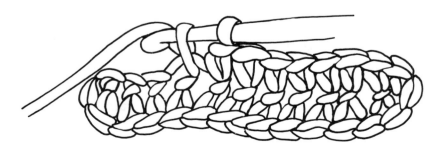

To Work Round 1 of Rectangle

Before You Begin a Project

In some sense, the most critical moments in the making of a project occur before you ever crochet a stitch of it. Selecting and beginning a project take thought and planning, and the more carefully you lay the groundwork, the more successful and enjoyable your work will be.

When you find a project you think you'd like, carefully read the entire set of instructions to find out what's involved. If you are unfamiliar with some of the stitches or skills the project requires, you'll be able to find information in "Crochet Stitches and Skills" that will show you how to proceed. Try out any new stitches or techniques in a sample swatch before committing yourself to the project. Does the project require substantial blocking? If so, don't select it without being prepared to block it, following the instructions on blocking in the section on "Finishing Techniques," or you won't be happy with the final result. Is the project joined at completion or is it joined as you work? Is the size right for your needs, and if not, can it be adjusted? Even the weather might influence your decision: Choose a lightweight cotton project for those hot summer days on the beach, and save that heavy wool afghan for winter evenings in front of the television. The variety of possible motif projects is extensive enough to ensure that somewhere in this book is the right project for you to make right now—and as you look for it, you can line up other projects for the future. A look at each part of the project format will help you make the best decision.

Approximate Finished Size

If you make the same number of motifs as the instructions tell you to and arrange them in the same manner, and if your gauge matches that in the instructions (see "Gauge" below), your project will be more or less the size given "as shown." (Individual differences in tension will always produce slight variations in size.) However, many motif projects are easily adjustable. The finished size of such projects can be any multiple of the size of one motif. Make more motifs and you have a larger project; make fewer and it will be smaller. How you arrange the motifs of such projects will determine the shape of the finished piece. The same number of motifs across and down will make a square; add more in one direction and you'll have a rectangle. Thus, any of the projects in which the size is given as adjustable can be adapted to any desired size, from a baby blanket (or even a pillow) to a bedspread. If a project is adjustable, the instructions will tell you so, and will tell you, as well, the size of the unit by which it can be adjusted.

The size of the border must be included in the measurements of a finished project. The size given for the border in the instructions is for the total number of inches it adds to the length or width of the project. That is, if a border is 3 inches wide, the instructions will tell you to add 6 inches to both the width and the length.

Degree of Difficulty

Getting in over your head is a guaranteed way to take the fun out of a craft project. If you're not certain whether or not a project is too difficult, make a sample motif—a good idea in any event—and see how it goes. If you haven't worked with a particular technique, such as tapestry stitch or openwork, select one of the easier designs to make first and save the more difficult for another time. Don't be misled by the appearance of a project; many quite easy motif designs look difficult. Go instead by the designation in the instructions and by your own evaluation of the project after reading through it. Don't feel, either, that you must constantly work to the upper limit of your crocheting ability. Even the most experienced crocheters enjoy working on easy designs. I usually have two projects going at the same time, one that requires skill and concentration, another that I can do while watching television, when at least part of my mind is elsewhere and I can let my fingers do the necessary thinking.

Yarn

It has been a delight to select the beautiful yarns in this book from the vast array of those available today, and I am very grateful to the yarn companies and their representatives who have generously and courteously supplied the yarns I have used. Since the projects in this book have been designed using these yarns, I urge you to use the specific yarn listed in the project instructions. You will find brand name, color, and color number listed. You needn't, of course, follow my color choices. Every yarn selected for this book comes in such a stunning array of colors that it was frequently all I could do to settle on one set of colors rather than another. However, if at all possible, do not substitute one brand for another.

All the yarns used in this book are nationally available. If you can't find a particular yarn in your area, write to the yarn company (see "Yarn Buying Guide" for addresses) for information on mail-order buying and/or availability in your area.

If you must substitute another brand of yarn, it is absolutely essential that you make a large sample, block it, and check it for gauge, texture, and appearance. Even yarns of the same weight will have individual characteristics that can affect every aspect of your project.

Other Materials
Crochet requires little else beyond a hook and some yarn. Perhaps the only other necessity for motif crochet is a yarn needle to sew motifs together. A yarn needle is about two to three inches long, with a large eye and a blunt point so that you won't pierce and split the yarn. You will also need a tape measure and equipment for blocking, which is listed separately in the section on blocking in "Finishing Techniques." If you plan to use your crocheted piece as a pillow or a framed wall hanging, you will need special materials. Pillow materials are listed in the instructions when appropriate; framing materials are described in the section on framed crochet in "Finishing Techniques."

Gauge
Gauge is the size of the stitches measured in number of stitches per square inch. Your gauge depends on the yarn, the size of the hook you use, and the tension you maintain on the yarn while crocheting. Before you begin a project, always make a sample and compare your gauge to that given in the instructions.

Gauge is usually given in terms of the number of stitches per inch and the number of rows per inch. When this is the case, make a swatch at least 4 inches square in the appropriate pattern stitch. For example, if the gauge is 4 stitches = 1 inch and 3 rows = 1 inch, work 12 rows of 16 stitches each. Your swatch should measure 4 inches square. In this book, gauge is frequently given as the size of one motif. In that case, make and measure a motif.

If your gauge is different from the gauge given in the instructions, both the finished size and the texture of your project will also be different. *More* stitches per square inch will result in a stiffer fabric and smaller finished size; *fewer* stitches per square inch will produce a looser fabric and larger finished size.

If you aren't concerned with matching the finished size of your project to that given and you like the texture of your sample, you needn't adjust your gauge. However, if you want to adjust your gauge to that given, the easiest way to do so is to change the size of the hook you are using. If your sample swatch or motif is smaller than the size given, use a larger hook; if your sample is larger, use a smaller hook.

Working Instructions

The instructions in this book are written to conform with the "Simplified Instructions" developed in 1979 by a committee of professionals from yarn companies and major consumer publications. The standardization of instructions is an enormous benefit to all of us who write and follow crochet and knitting instructions. Whenever you see the "Simplified Instructions" logo, you will know that these standard abbreviations and measurements have been followed.

Note

If a project requires a special stitch or technique, the "Note" before the actual working instructions will provide instructions or will tell you how to find instructions elsewhere in the book.

Finishing Techniques

To Hide Yarn Tails

Each time that you change yarn or fasten off, one or two yarn tails will be left hanging on the side of your piece. Don't wait until the project is completed to hide these tails. You will have a much better sense of how the piece looks after the tails are hidden, and you won't face the unpleasant task of having to weave in a multitude of tails at one time.

To work over tails: If you are changing yarns, and if you are working the next row with the front of the piece facing you, the easiest way to hide yarn tails is to hold them behind the heads of the stitches and work around them in the same way that yarn is carried behind the work in tapestry stitch. (See "To Change and Carry Yarn in Tapestry-Stitch Designs," p. 23.)

To weave in tails: Work with a blunt yarn needle or a crochet hook a few sizes smaller than the hook used to make the piece. With the wrong side of the piece facing you, draw the yarn tail through the back vertical loops of successive stitches until it is hidden.

To Join Motifs

To join through opposing pairs of stitches: Most of the motifs in this book are worked from the inside out and therefore automatically have a round of stitches on the outer edge when completed. Such a finished outer edge is very helpful when joining motifs, so if the pieces are worked back and forth, the instructions may tell you to add an edging round of single crochet before joining, or to join motifs in some other manner.

When two motifs with finished edges are placed side by side, the heads of the stitches of the outside rounds line up in opposing pairs. Each pair has four loops, two from each stitch, that can be used for joining. The instructions will tell you whether to join the pieces with the front sides or wrong sides facing you, and whether to join with a slip stitch or single crochet, or to sew the motifs together. When only two loops are used for joining, usually they are the two, called the back loops, that lie next to each other in the center of the four loops. Join with yarn the same color as the outside rounds. When joining motifs of different colors, the instructions may tell you to use one color or the other; if not, either is acceptable. If you are sewing the motifs together, use a blunt two- to three-inch yarn needle and work carefully through the loops, trying not to pierce the yarn.

To join as you work: Openwork motifs, for the most part, have uneven, lacy edges that are unsuitable for stitch-by-stitch joining. Instead, joining is incorporated into the final round of each motif. When one motif is completed, and when the second has reached the last few repeats of the final round, the instructions will tell you to work back and forth between the outer points of the completed motif and the one you are making in such a way that, when the second motif is completed, the two are joined. Usually the outer point of the completed motif consists of a loop a few chains long, called a picot. When you reach the outer point of the motif you are joining, you will chain out from it, slip stitch into the picot of the opposing point of the completed motif, chain back to the original point, and continue working around the motif. The instructions will tell you precisely how to proceed. Make sure that the front of the completed motif is facing up and that you are working into the correct set of outer points of the completed motif. The instructions will tell you how many points of the completed motifs should be left empty at the top and bottom as you make your chain of motifs. When the first chain of motifs is the proper length, you will begin another, joining each motif in this chain not only to the motif next to it but to the one above it as well, and will continue in this manner until all the motifs have been joined.

Openwork designs almost always require small secondary motifs, called fills, to give the piece structure and to complete the design. If you examine a piece of openwork after all the large motifs have been completed, you will see circular holes between each set of four motifs. A fill is joined to the unused points of the four surrounding motifs, and often to the slip-stitch joins between motifs as well. When adding a fill, don't try to work into these joins; instead, slip stitch around them.

To Block Crochet
The ultimate success of a motif crochet project frequently rests upon how professionally its pieces are blocked. Many kinds of crochet are distorted and uneven until after blocking. Since most motif designs depend for their effect on uniformly geometric shapes, these distortions have more impact than usual. If the instructions tell you that a project requires blocking and you are not prepared to do so, find another project—there are many—in which blocking is optional or not required. But rather than avoid blocking, I urge you to make it central to your crochet work. The difference in appearance between blocked and unblocked crochet is often the *only* difference between the professional handmade look and the sloppy, slightly misshapen look of the homemade.

You'll need a blocking board or cork board, a right angle, a transparent straight edge and/or tape measure, pushpins, and a good steam iron. A long metal straight edge—they come as long as six feet—is a help for large projects. Frequently, graph paper or a paper pattern is useful.

Your blocking board must be made of a substance that will hold pushpins. The cork board used for bulletin boards is the most easily available. Don't buy a bulletin board with an outer frame because you'll want to be able to put several boards together to block large projects. If you have the space, a cork-topped pattern-making table is the ideal blocking board.

Pin the pieces to the board with pushpins, following the measurements given in the instructions. Use the straight edge and right angle to square the corners and make the sides straight. If you are blocking many small squares, you can save time by drawing squares of the correct size on graph paper (leave some room between squares to facilitate pinning), putting the graph paper over the blocking board, and pinning the motifs to the board on the outlines you have drawn. Set your steam iron to the highest setting, and, when it is ready, hold it over the pinned piece of crochet about two inches away. *Never* let the iron touch the crocheted fabric or your piece will lose all its texture and the yarn will be damaged. If your iron has a "puff-of-steam" feature, one or two good puffs will block a small motif.

Notice that I don't put a towel on the crocheted fabric and then steam through it. The method I use is more like that used in dressmaking. I prefer it because you can see what you're doing, because the steaming goes much faster, and because the towel method usually requires some contact between the iron and the towel to work well. Any contact between the iron and the crocheted piece, even with a towel between them, risks disaster. If your iron drips, put a piece of unbleached muslin over the crocheted piece before you begin—the steam will go right through it.

All is not lost if you don't have a steam iron. A friend of mine who found himself without a steam iron came up with this clever solution: he pinned his motifs to the blocking board, then stood the board at one end of his shower covered in a plastic tarp, pointed the shower nozzle away from the board, turned on the shower to its hottest setting, and let the steam from the shower do the rest.

Whatever steaming method you use, a little steam, just enough to slightly dampen the piece, is plenty. You don't want to get the piece actually wet. After steaming, the piece must dry in place for as long as possible. Overnight is usually sufficient. Test to see whether the piece has "set" by removing a few pushpins and watching what happens. If the piece stays put, it can be unpinned.

If you need to block a large finished afghan and can't fit it all on your board or boards, you can block it a little at a time. Pin as much as possible to the board, block it, let it dry, unpin it, and move a new section of it on to the blocking board. When working in this manner, you must always pin all the way around the section being blocked, which means that you'll be pinning down the middle of the piece as well as pinning the edges.

If you have cats, dogs, children, or simply a tendency to spill coffee, always cover the pieces being blocked with a waterproof piece of fabric or lightweight piece of plastic.

To Make a Pillow
Measure your completed crocheted pillow front. Cut two pieces of color-coordinated fabric ½ inch larger than the pillow front to allow for a ¼-inch seam around the pillow. Pin the pieces of fabric together with the wrong sides out and sew the pieces together by hand or machine, leaving a ¼-inch seam allowance. It is a good idea to reinforce the corners with an extra row of stitches set as close as possible to the first because the seam allowance will be trimmed at the corners. Don't close the pillow completely; leave a 4- to 5-inch opening in the middle of one side. Cut the seam allowance diagonally across the corners, turn the pillow inside out, and push the corners out to form sharp points. (If they don't, you haven't cut off enough seam allowance.) Stuff the pillow with polyester stuffing. You will need about one pound of stuffing per square foot of pillow. Sew the opening closed with a slip stitch, turning under the seam allowance as you work. Pin the pillow front to one side of the pillow and, from the other side, sew it to the seam of the pillow with a slip stitch or blind stitch so that the stitches will not show on the crocheted front of the pillow.

Framed Crochet
Motif designs, particularly quilt patterns, are striking when framed. You will need a frame of the appropriate size, including glass and cardboard backing, a piece of thin cardboard, and glue designated for use with fabric. Cut the cardboard to the size of the crocheted piece and carefully glue the piece to it. Use as little glue as possible and make sure it doesn't come through the fabric to the front. After the glue has dried, the design is ready to be put in the frame according to the instructions accompanying the frame.

To Frame Large Projects
Large designs in lightweight yarn, such as the Nine-Patch Afghan, can be handled much as a small design except that you must make your own frame or have one made for you. You will need a large piece of wallboard, a piece of thin Plexiglas the same size, four very large screws with ornamental heads, a drill and drill bit of the appropriate size for the screws, and some means of hanging the quite-heavy completed piece on your wall. Some very large screws of the molly-bolt

type are long enough to go through Plexiglas, wallboard, and wall. In general, look for the kind of apparatus used to hang heavy mirrors. You will need, as well, glue designated for use with fabric and a long straight edge and a right angle.

Have both wallboard and Plexiglas cut at least a few inches larger than the crocheted piece. They must be larger because you are going to attach them to each other with large screws and you don't want to make holes in your fabric. However, how much larger they are is up to you and will depend on the size of your wall and how large a border you prefer. Put the Plexiglas on top of the wallboard and drill four holes, one in each corner, through both pieces at the same time. Remove the Plexiglas and use the straight edge and right angle to draw an outline of the crocheted piece on the wallboard. Make sure that the outline is centered on the wallboard *exactly* as you wish the crocheted piece to be. You are now ready to glue the crocheted piece to the wall-board. You will need to crosshatch the wallboard with glue; putting it around only the edges is insufficient. Depending on how quickly your glue dries, you may want to put all the glue on at once and then set the piece in place, or work from the top down, adding glue, and finally unfolding the piece on to the surface a little at a time. Allow the glue to dry thoroughly and then screw the Plexiglas tightly in place. The pressure between wallboard and Plexiglas will help hold the shape of the piece. You are now ready to hang the piece on your wall.

II

Squares

Nine-Patch Afghan

Approximate finished size: 50-inch square
No experience necessary

Quilters vary a basic pattern such as the Nine-Patch not only by the color of the squares that compose the design but by their size and fabric as well. You can do the same thing with the basic crocheted square. If you would like a larger or smaller afghan, simply add or subtract a row or two from each basic square. If you prefer a heavier afghan, or if you simply want your work to go faster, use a heavier-weight yarn. Each yarn, of course, will require a different number of rows to reach a given size, and each will add its own special look and texture to the design.

Materials:
Phildar Luxe 025, 50-gram skeins:
   6 skeins color 71, océan (dark blue)
   6 skeins color 03, angelot (light blue)
   3 skeins color 11, bois de rose (dusty rose)
   3 skeins color 68, nymphette (peach)
   Small amount color 96, violette (lavender)
   Small amount color 29, bruyère (plum)
Steel crochet hook, size 0
Yarn needle

Gauge: 1 full square = 3-inch square

Note: Instructions for the basic square, half-square, and quarter-square are given in "Basic Geometric Shapes." Instructions for the single-crochet post stitch and the reverse single crochet are given in "Terms and Techniques."

Full squares: Make 84 in dark blue, 44 in light blue, 8 in dusty rose, 4 in peach, 4 in lavender, and 1 in plum. Follow the instructions for the basic square until you have completed 9 rounds. There will be 16 stitches between corner stitches on each side of the square.

Half-squares: Make 32 in dark blue. Follow the instructions for the basic half-square until you have completed 9 rows. There will be 16 stitches between corner stitches on each side.

Quarter-squares: Make 4 in dark blue. Follow the instructions for the basic quarter-square until you have completed 9 rows. There will be 18 stitches in the last row.

Finishing: Block the squares and partial squares to 3 inches on each side. With the wrong side facing you and working through the *two back loops only* of opposing pairs of stitches, sew the squares together. Follow the placement diagram for the position of each color. Fill in the outer edges with half-squares and add a quarter-square to each corner.

Border: With dusty rose, work 8 rounds of single crochet around entire joined piece, working 3 single crochets in each corner. Change to peach and work 24 more rounds in the same manner. *Next round:* Work in single-crochet post stitch, working (1 sc post st, ch 2, 1 sc post st) in corners. *Next round:* Work in reverse single crochet. Fasten off.

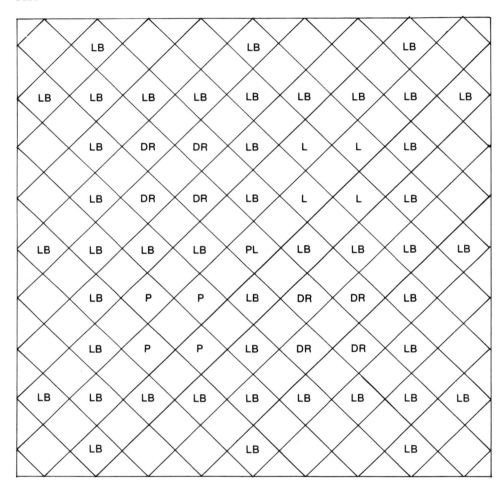

**Nine-Patch Afghan
Motif-Placement Diagram**

Key
Empty squares = dark blue
PL = plum
P = peach
DR = dusty rose
L = lavender
LB = light blue

Checkerboard Squares Pillow

Approximate finished size: 20-inch square
No experience needed

Many patchwork quilt designs are composed entirely of squares of the same size. The pattern of these quilts comes from the color selected for each square. This is a lucky break for the crocheter, who can re-create these surprisingly modern yet deeply traditional designs simply by making the most basic of crocheted motifs, the square. I hope you'll want to design or adapt a favorite quilt pattern of your own after you see how easy it is. Incidentally, the traditional name for this Amish design, Checkerboard Squares, is somewhat misleading. Neither the diagonal placement of the squares nor the mix of colors resembles our idea of a checkerboard.

Materials:
Phildar Luxe 025, 50-gram skeins:
   1 skein color 29, bruyère (plum)
   1 skein color 68, nymphette (peach)
   About ½ skein color 71, océan (dark blue)
   About ½ skein color 03, angelot (light blue)
   About ¼ skein color 11, bois de rose (dusty rose)
Steel crochet hook, size 0
Yarn needle
For pillow form:
   Two 20½-inch squares of fabric, color-coordinated with yarn
   Sewing thread to match fabric
   Polyester stuffing

Gauge: 1 square = 2-inch square

Note: Instructions for the basic square, half-square, and quarter-square are given in "Basic Geometric Shapes." Instructions for making and stuffing a pillow form are given in "Finishing Techniques."

Squares: Make 21 in peach, 16 in dark blue, 12 in light blue, 8 in dusty rose, and 4 in plum. Follow the instructions for the basic square until you have completed 6 rounds. There will be 10 stitches between corner stitches on each side of the square.

Half-squares: Make 20 in peach. Follow the instructions for the half-square until you have completed 6 rows. There will be 10 stitches between corner stitches.

Quarter-squares: Make 4 in peach. Follow the instructions for the quarter-square until you have completed 6 rows. There will be 12 stitches in the last row.

Finishing: Block squares and partial squares to 2 inches on each side. With the wrong sides facing you and working through the *back loops only* of opposing pairs of stitches, sew the squares together. Follow the placement diagram for the position of each color. Fill in the outside edges with half-squares and add a quarter-square to each corner.

Border: With peach, work 1 round of single crochet around entire joined piece, working 3 single crochet in each corner. With plum, work 11 more rounds of single crochet in the same manner.

Final finishing: Block the crocheted pillow. Make and stuff a 20-inch pillow form and sew the crocheted piece to one side of it.

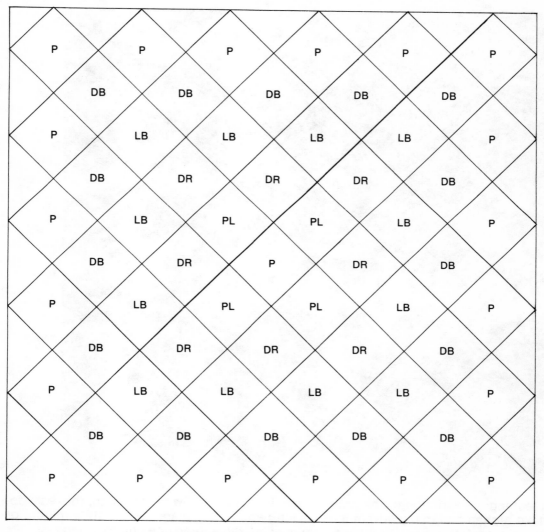

**Checkerboard Squares Pillow
Motif-Placement Diagram**

Key
P = peach
PL = plum
DR = dusty rose
LB = light blue
DB = dark blue

Puffy Squares Afghan

Approximate finished size: 42 by 60 inches
No experience necessary

A rectangular variation of the Amish Sunshine-and-Shadow quilt design, this easy-to-make afghan has many advantages—each two-round square takes only a minute or two to complete, no partial squares are needed, the joining goes quickly because it is crocheted instead of sewn, and, best of all, no blocking is required.

Materials:
Lily 4-ply Sugar 'n' Cream:
    6 skeins color 26, light blue
    4 skeins color 42, tea rose
    3 skeins color 46, rose pink
    2 skeins color 3, cream
    2 skeins color 99, raspberry
    2 skeins color 28, delft blue
    1 skein color 48, mauve
Crochet hook, size H

Gauge: 1 square = 2¼-inch square

Design tip: You'll enjoy this project more if you don't set out to make all 130 light blue squares at one time, then all 98 tea rose, and so on, waiting to join them until after completing all 438 squares. Instead, begin at the center of the design: make 6 cream and 14 tea rose squares and join them. Then make the 18 rose pink squares that come next, and join those. Each time that you join a new color, you'll feel a sense of accomplishment and enjoy the new interplay of colors. Watching the quilt grow in this way will keep your interest and energy high.

Squares: Make 130 in light blue, 98 in tea rose, 56 in rose pink, 40 in cream, 42 in raspberry, 50 in delft blue, and 22 in mauve. Ch 4.
Rnd 1: 15 dc in fourth ch from hook—16 dc. Join with sl st to top ch of ch-4.
Rnd 2: Work in back loops of sts *only.* Ch 1, (1 sc, ch 2, 1 sc) in first st, *1 sc in each of next 3 sts, (1 sc, ch 2, 1 sc) in next st. Rep from * twice, 1 sc in each of last 3 sts. Join with sl st to first sc. Fasten off.

Finishing: With the wrong sides of the squares facing you, join the squares with a sl st through the *two back loops only.* Follow the color photograph for the position of each color.

Edging: With the front side facing you, attach light blue in left-hand corner of any corner square. Work in *back loops of sts only.* [(1 sl st, ch 2, 1 sl st) in ch-2 sp, 1 sl st in each of next 5 sts, *(1 sl st, ch 2, 1 sl st) in ch-2 sp, 1 sl st in each of next 5 sts, 1 dec in last st of square and first st of next square, 1 sl st in each of next 5 sts. Rep from * across side.] Rep within brackets 3 times. Join with sl st to first sl st. Fasten off.

Granny Floor Pillow

Approximate finished size: Adjustable to any multiple of 8½ inches before border rounds. Size as shown is 28-inch square.
No experience necessary

Granny square designs offer an unequaled chance to play with color. Traditionally, the multicolored inner rounds are completed with an outer round or rounds that remain constant in color throughout. But other possibilities abound: Every square can be of the same color, colors can go from light to dark or vice versa, or the centers can be the same and the outer rounds different. There's no better way to start designing your own projects than with the granny square. So open your yarn closet, collect all your odds and ends, and join an American tradition.

Materials:
Reynolds Town and Country, 50-gram skeins:
   2 skeins color 227 (dark green)
   1 skein color 228 (light green)
   About ½ skein color 247 (salmon)
   About ½ skein color 270 (lavender)
   About ½ skein color 203 (plum)
   About ½ skein color 248 (apricot)
Crochet hook, size G
Yarn needle
For pillow form:
   Two 28½-inch squares of dark green fabric
   Sewing thread to match fabric
   Polyester stuffing

Gauge: 2 rounds in granny square pattern = 2½ inches

Note: Instructions for full and partial granny squares are given in "Basic Geometric Shapes." Instructions for adjusting the size of a project and making a pillow form are given in "Finishing Techniques."

Granny squares and partial squares: Make 13 full squares, 8 half-squares, and 4 quarter-squares. Follow the instructions for granny squares and partial granny squares until you have completed 5 rounds or rows. The first 3 rounds are worked in combinations of salmon, lavender, apricot, and plum. Follow the placement diagram for the position of colors within each square. Round 4 is always light green and Round 5 is always dark green.

Finishing: With the wrong sides facing you, sew or crochet the squares together through the *two back loops only* of opposing pairs of stitches.

Border: Attach dark green in any corner. Ch 3 (counts as 1 dc), 2 dc in ch-2 corner sp, ch 2, 3 dc in same corner, [ch 1, skip next ch-5 sp (which is same color as corner), *(3 dc, ch 1) in each of next 3 sps, skip next (dark green) sp, 3 dc in ch-2 corner of full square, ch 1, skip next (dark green) sp, (3 dc, ch 1) in each of next 3 sps, skip next sp (same color as next ch-4 ring), (3 dc, ch 1) in ch-4 ring, skip next sp (same color as ring), rep from * twice, ending last rep with skip last sp (same color as corner), (3 dc, ch 2, 3 dc) in corner]. Rep within brackets twice, ch 1, skip next ch-5 sp, rep from * on last side, ending with skip last sp. Join with sl st to top of starting ch-3.

Rnd 2: Sl st to ch-2 corner sp. Work round in granny square pattern. *Note:* If you would prefer a wider border, simply continue to work in granny square pattern for as many rounds as desired.

Finishing: No blocking is needed. Make and stuff a 28-inch-square pillow and sew the crocheted pillow front to one side of it.

Motif-Placement Diagram cells (reading in diagonal lattice order):

Top corner squares: 1. S / 2. L / 3. A — 1. A / 2. S / 3. P — 1. L / 2. A / 3. S — 1. L / 2. A / 3. P

1. P / 2. L / 3. S — 1. S / 2. P / 3. L — 1. P / 2. L / 3. A

1. A / 2. P / 3. L — 1. L / 2. S / 3. A — 1. A / 2. P / 3. S — 1. A / 2. S / 3. L

1. S / 2. L / 3. P — 1. A / 2. S / 3. L — 1. A / 2. S / 3. P

1. A / 2. L / 3. S — 1. P / 2. A / 3. L — 1. S / 2. P / 3. A — 1. S / 2. P / 3. L

1. L / 2. P / 3. A — 1. L / 2. S / 3. P — 1. L / 2. A / 2. A

1. A / 2. S / 3. L — 1. S / 2. A / 3. L — 1. A / 2. P / 3. S — 1. L / 2. S / 3. A

**Granny Floor Pillow
Motif-Placement Diagram**

Key
A = apricot
S = salmon
L = lavender
P = plum

Granny Sunshine-and-Shadow Afghan

Approximate finished size: 52-inch square
No experience needed

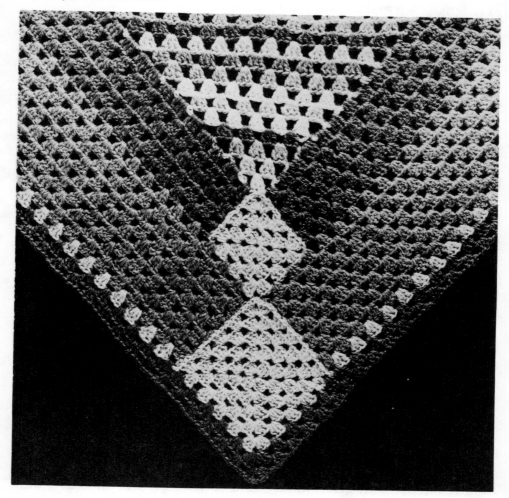

Perhaps the most popular of all motif crochet, granny squares are an American creation, developed by nineteenth-century women to use up leftover yarn in the same way that patchwork quilts were developed to scraps of fabric. So it seems particularly appropriate to combine these two crafts in this granny adaptation of a well-known Amish patchwork quilt design. If this were a quilt, every three-double-crochet group would be made of a different piece of fabric. Happily, crocheters can adapt these imaginative designs to a technique as quick and easy as the granny square. Incidentally, the solid squares in the corners of the borders are a traditional element of Amish quilt designs.

Materials:
Reynolds Town and Country, 50-gram skeins
   5 skeins color 227 (dark green)
   4 skeins color 203 (plum)
   2 skeins color 270 (lavender)
   1 skein color 228 (light green)
   1 skein color 247 (salmon)
   1 skein color 248 (apricot)
Crochet hook, size G
Yarn needle

Gauge: 2 rounds = 2-inch square

Note: Sometimes when a granny square design requires a particularly stretchable square, a ch-3 is worked at the corners instead of a ch-2. This is just such a situation. To make the center square, follow the instructions for the basic granny square in "Basic Geometric Shapes," *but* work (3 dc, *ch 3*, 3 dc) at each corner.

Center square: Work in the granny square pattern for 16 rounds in this color sequence: *Rnd 1:* light green; *Rnd 2:* dark green; *Rnd 3:* lavender; *Rnd 4:* apricot; *Rnd 5:* lavender; *Rnd 6:* salmon; *Rnd 7:* dark green; *Rnd 8:* light green; *Rnd 9:* plum; *Rnd 10:* apricot; *Rnd 11:* salmon; *Rnd 12:* lavender; *Rnd 13:* plum; *Rnd 14:* salmon; *Rnd 15:* light green; *Rnd 16:* dark green. Round 16 is the last complete round. From now on you will no longer work in rounds, but in rows on one side of the square at a time.
Row 1: Attach light green in any ch-3 corner. Ch 4 (counts as 1 dc, ch 1), *3 dc in next ch-1 sp, ch 1. Rep from * across the side of the square, ending with 1 dc in ch-3 corner.
Row 2: Attach apricot in ch-4 sp and then rep Row 1, ending with 1 dc in last ch-1 sp. Fasten off. The side has decreased by one (3 dc, ch 1) group.
Rows 3–15: Rep Row 2. Work in the following color sequence: *Row 3:* lavender; *Row 4:* salmon; *Row 5:* plum; *Row 6:* light green; *Row 7:* dark green; *Row 8:* salmon; *Row 9:* apricot; *Row 10:* lavender; *Row*

11: apricot; *Row 12:* plum; *Row 13:* salmon; *Row 14:* lavender; *Row 15:* apricot. The side will decrease by one (3 dc, ch 1) group each row. Row 15 will have only one group.
Rep Rows 1 to 15 on the remaining three sides of the square.

Block: Block the center square to a 30-inch square.

Inner border: The inner border is worked back and forth in rows on one side of the square at a time.
Row 1: Attach plum in ch-4 sp to the left of any 3-dc corner group. Ch 3 (counts as 1 dc), 2 dc in ch-4 sp, *ch 1, 3 dc in next ch-1 sp. Rep from * across side, ending with 3 dc in last ch-1 sp before corner, turn.
Row 2: Ch 4 (counts as 1 dc, ch 1), *3 dc in ch-1 sp, ch 1. Rep from * across row, ending with 1 dc in last dc of previous row, turn.
Row 3: Ch 3 (counts as 1 dc), 2 dc in ch-1 sp, *ch 1, 3 dc in next ch-1 sp. Rep from * across row, ending with 3 dc in ch-4 sp, turn.
Rows 4 and 5: Rep Rows 2 and 3. At the end of Row 5, fasten off.
Rep Rows 1 to 5 on the remaining three sides of the square.

Make and join inner corner squares: Make four squares in lavender, following the instructions for the basic granny square worked in one color for three rounds. With the wrong sides facing you, sew the corner squares to the border.

Outer border: The outer border is worked back and forth in rows on one side of the square at a time.
Row 1: Attach dark green in any ch-2 corner. Ch 4 (counts as 1 dc, ch 1), *3 dc in next ch-1 sp, ch 1. Rep from * across side, ending with 1 dc in ch-2 corner, turn.
Row 2: Work as you did Row 3 of the inner border.
Row 3: Work as you did Row 2 of the inner border.
Rows 4 to 8: Rep these two rows (Rows 2 and 3). At the end of Row 8, fasten off.
Rep Rows 1 to 8 on the remaining three sides of the square.

Make and join outer corner squares: Make four squares in lavender, following the instructions for the basic granny square worked in one color for five rounds. Join as you did the inner corner squares.

Edging: Attach lavender in any ch-2 corner and work one round of the granny square pattern around the entire afghan. Change to plum and work two more rounds. Fasten off.

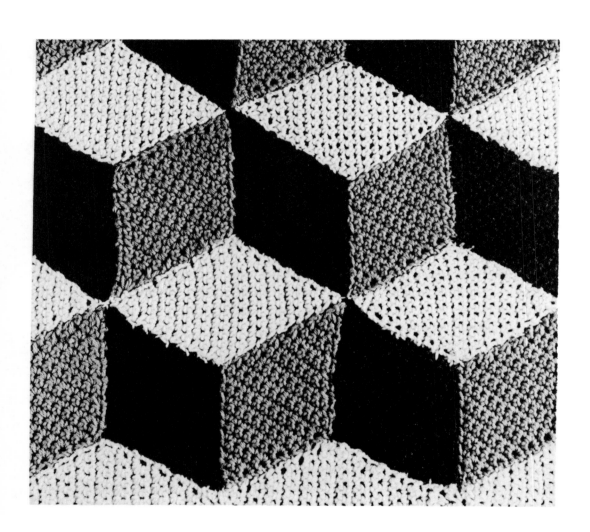

III

Other Geometric Shapes

Sunflower Hot Pad

Approximate finished size: 8½-inch diameter
Average experience necessary

This simple hexagon design is so bold and bright, it is almost a shame to cover up with a hot dish. Made in only one thickness (two are used here to provide extra protection for your table) and perhaps a thinner yarn, it would work well sewn to a pillow, a placemat, or even the back of potholder. Worked in perle cotton, it would also be a charming appliqué for a sweater or jacket.

Materials:
Lily 4-ply Sugar 'n' Cream:
   ½ skein color 28, delft blue
   ½ skein color 62, emerald green
   Small amount color 21, shrimp
Crochet hook, size G

Gauge: 2-round hexagon = 2 inches in diameter

Hexagons: Make 12 with delft blue and 2 with shrimp. Hexagons will be joined in pairs to provide extra thickness. Ch 4.
Rnd 1: 11 dc in fourth ch from hook—12 dc. Join with sl st to top of starting ch.
Rnd 2: Ch 1, 1 sc in first st, *3 sc in next st, 1 sc in next st. Rep from * 4 times, 3 sc in last st. Join with sl st to first sc. Fasten off.

Join pairs of hexagons: Hold two hexagons of the same color back to back. Attach yarn of same color through the two back loops of any pair of opposing corner sts. Ch 1, working through the *two back loops only* of opposing pairs of stitches, *work 3 sc in corner sts, 1 sc in each of next 3 pairs of sts. Rep from * 5 times. Join with sl st to first sc. Fasten off. Make six double-thickness hexagons of delft blue and one of shrimp.

Join outer round of hexagons: With the fronts of two delft blue hexagons facing you, attach delft blue through the two *front* loops only of any set of corner sts. Working in two *front* loops *only*, sl st through corner sts, each pair of next 5 sts, and next set of corner sts. Ch 1 and turn the motifs over. Working down the other side of the pieces, sl st through the two remaining loops (back loops) of each pair of sts. Fasten off. Join the remaining delft blue hexagons so that you make a circle. After a hexagon has been joined to its two adjacent hexagons, it should have one inner edge and three outer edges empty. The sixth hexagon will be joined to both the fifth and the first.

Join center hexagon: With front sides facing you and with delft blue, sl st through *both* loops of shrimp center hexagon and the *back loop only* of the opposing sts of the outer round.

Leaves: Because the leaves are curved, the front piece and the back piece of each leaf must be worked in reverse order. With emerald green, make two of Side A and two of Side B.

Side A: Ch 12.

Rnd 1: 1 sl st in second ch from hook, 1 sc in next ch, 1 hdc in next ch, 1 dc in next ch, 2 dc in next ch, (1 tr in next ch, 2 tr in next ch) twice, 1 tr in next ch, (1 dc, 1 hdc, 1 sl st) in last ch, ch 2. Working in other side of ch, 1 dc in same ch, 1 tr in each of next 3 chs, (1 tr, 1 dc) in next ch, 1 dc in next ch, 1 hdc in next ch, 1 sc in next ch, 1 sl st in each of last 2 chs. Fasten off.

Side B: Ch 12.

Rnd 1: 1 sl st in each of first 2 chs from hook, 1 sc in next ch, 1 hdc in next ch, 1 dc in next ch, (1 dc, 1 tr) in next ch, 1 tr in each of next 3 chs, 1 dc in next ch, (1 dc, ch 2, 1 sl st) in last ch, ch 1, (1 hdc, 1 dc) in same ch, (1 tr in next ch, 2 tr in next ch) twice, 1 tr in next ch, 2 dc in next ch, 1 dc in next ch, 1 hdc in next ch, 1 sc in next ch, 1 sl st in last ch. Fasten off.

Join leaves, stem, and flower: You are now going to join the two pieces of each leaf, make a stem, and attach the leaves and stem to the flower all at the same time. Arrange the two pieces of each leaf back to back. The left-hand leaf has Side A facing front; the right-hand leaf has Side B facing front. With emerald green, ch 35. Sl st through the bottom ch sps of both pieces of the left-hand leaf, sl st through all 4 loops of pairs of sts to top of leaf, 1 sl st in top, ch 1, 1 sl st through far left corner of left bottom hexagon (see photograph for placement), sl st through all 4 loops of each pair of sts on other side of leaf to bottom ch-sp, sl st in each of next 16 chs of stem, ch 5, sl st through bottom ch-sps of right-hand leaf pieces, sl st around this leaf, joining it as you did the other to the hexagon. When you reach the bottom ch-sp, sl st in each of 5 chs. Making sure that neither stem nor leaf is twisted, work 1 sl st in each of last chs, 1 sl st on right side of center hexagon-join, ch 1, 1 sl st on left side of hexagon-join and first ch of stem. Fasten off.

Giant Rainbow Ball

Approximate finished size: 42-inch diameter
No experience necessary

Children love this big, bright ball. Its giant size and very light weight make it especially fun for small children, and its brilliant colors make store-bought beach balls look drab. It will get so much use, you'll want to be able to wash it, so after you join the two halves, don't hide the yarn tail completely. Then, when necessary, you can easily take the ball apart, machine-wash and dry it, then reassemble it.

Materials:
Berella "4" yarn by Bernat Yarn and Craft Corporation, 100-gram skeins:

    About ½ skein color 8933, scarlet
    About ½ skein color 8954, orange
    About ½ skein color 8903, canary
    About ½ skein color 8989, shannon green
    About ½ skein color 8967, marine blue
    About ½ skein color 8990, violet

Crochet hooks, sizes H and I
Yarn needle
For ball: Inflatable beach ball with 42-inch diameter

Note: Instructions for the triangle are given in "Basic Geometric Shapes."

Triangles: With I hook, make 2 with scarlet, 2 with orange, 2 with canary, 2 with shannon green, 2 with marine blue, and 2 with violet. Follow the instructions for the triangle until you have completed 34 rows. There will be 23 sts in the last row. At the end of the last row, ch 1 and work 1 sc in the side of every st to top of triangle—33 sts. Work 3 sc in top, 1 sc in side of every st, ending in side of last row—33 sts. Fasten off.

Join triangles: With wrong sides facing you, sew triangles together through the *two back loops only* of opposing pairs of stitches. Make two halves, each in the following color sequence: violet, marine blue, shannon green, canary, orange, scarlet. The scarlet triangle is joined to both the orange and violet.

Edge each half: With H hook and violet, work one round of single crochet around bottom of half. Change to marine blue and work one round. Change to shannon green and work final round. Fasten off. Repeat on other half.

Finishing: Partially inflate ball. Place crocheted ball around inner ball, matching the canary triangle on one half to the violet triangle on the other. With shannon green and H hook, sl st through all four loops of opposing pairs of stitches to join the two halves.

Climbing Blocks Afghan

Approximate finished size: Adjustable (width adjustable to any multiple of 7 inches plus 1 inch for border; length adjustable to any multiple of 10 inches plus 1 inch for border); as shown, 50 inches by 51 inches

No experience necessary

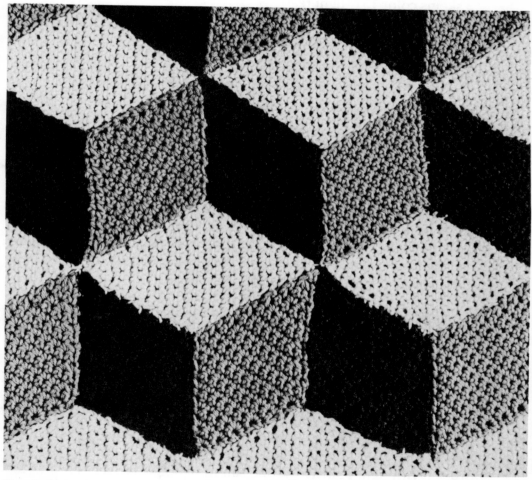

Nowhere is the stunning modernity of traditional quilt designs more apparent then in the classic Climbing Blocks pattern. It is composed always of three shades of diamonds—one dark, one medium, and one light—arranged so that the dark and medium diamonds appear as the sides of a cube and the light diamond as the top. However, the diamonds of each shade needn't be all of the same color, as they are here. Some wonderful Climbing Blocks variations employ as many as five or six colors in each shade group. So long as the colors in each group are distinctly light, medium, and dark, the visual illusion will succeed.

Materials:
Unger Utopia, 100-gram skeins:
   3 skeins color 131 (light teal)
   3 skeins color 133 (medium teal)
   3 skeins color 134 (dark teal)
Crochet hook, size I
Yarn needle

Gauge: 3 stitches = 1 inch; 7 rows = 2 inches

Note: Instructions for the diamond and triangle are given in "Basic Geometric Shapes." Instructions for the reverse single crochet are given in "Terms and Techniques."

Diamonds: Make 39 in light teal, 42 in medium teal, and 42 in dark teal. Follow the instructions for the diamond until you have completed 13 rows. Row 13 is an even row with 13 sts. Beginning with Row 14, follow the instructions for decreasing diamonds. Row 24 is the final row, consisting of a 3-st dec. Fasten off.

Triangles: Make 6 in light teal. Follow the instructions for triangles until you have completed 13 rows. There will be 13 sts in the last row. Fasten off.

Finishing: Follow the placement diagram for the position of diamonds and triangles. With wrong sides facing you, sew pieces together. Since pieces are not edged, work into the back vertical loops of the stitches. Work loosely, making sure that the points of the pieces match up.

Border: With light teal, work one round of single crochet around the entire joined piece, working 3 single crochet in corners and in points of diamonds at top and bottom and 3 single-crochet decreases between diamonds at top and bottom. Work final round in reverse single crochet.

Blocking: Block to 50 inches by 51 inches. *Note:* 51 inches is the measurement of the side of the piece. From the point of a diamond at the top to the point of a diamond at the bottom, it is 56 inches.

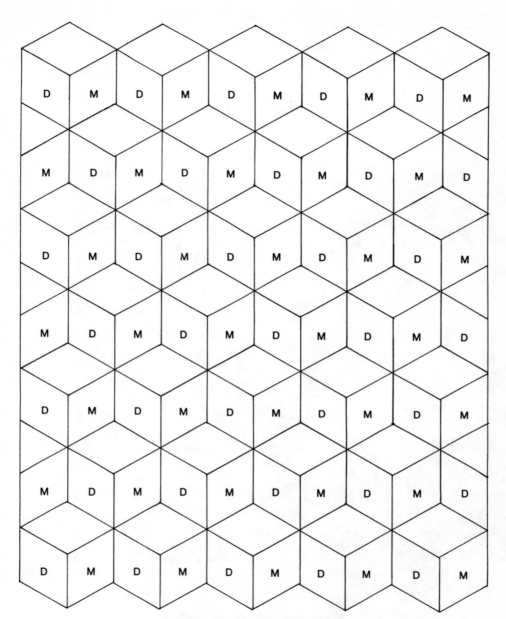

**Climbing Blocks Afghan
Motif-Placement Diagram**

Key Empty diamonds = light teal
M = medium teal
D = dark teal

Tumbling Blocks Afghan

Approximate finished size: Adjustable (width adjustable to any multiple of 6 inches plus 10 inches for border; length adjustable to any multiple of 10 inches plus 10 inches for border); as shown, 45 inches by 60 inches
Average experience necessary

This afghan, like Climbing Blocks, creates the illusion of three-dimensional boxes. But with squares for the tops of the boxes and diamonds for the sides, the cubes of Climbing Blocks are elongated into rectangular steps. Alternating light and dark blue for the tops produces the appearance of a series of steps moving diagonally across the afghan. Additional textural interest is provided by working the pieces in a simple single-crochet/double-crochet pattern. The lovely fabric this pattern creates has made it my favorite texture stitch. You'll see it again as the lush fabric of the Snowflakes Afghan. Try it for sweaters and baby clothes, too.

Materials:
Laines Anny Blatt #4, 50-gram skeins:
    7 skeins color 1566, copper
    3 skeins color 2302, aubergine (eggplant)
    3 skeins color 1297, bordeaux (dark red)
    3 skeins color 2303, aurore (light blue)
    3 skeins color 1290, ardoise (dark blue)
Crochet hook, size G
Yarn needle

Gauge: 4 stitches = 1 inch; 3 rows = 1 inch; square = 4½ inches on each side

Note: Instructions for the diamond are given in "Basic Geometric Shapes." Instructions for the reverse single crochet are given in "Terms and Techniques."

Pattern stitch:
Chain an even number.
Row 1: 1 sc in 2nd ch from hook, *1 dc in next ch, 1 sc in next ch. Rep from * across row. Ch 2, turn.
Row 2: 1 dc in first sc, *1 sc in next dc, 1 dc in next sc. Rep from * across row. Ch 1, turn.
Row 3: 1 sc in first dc, *1 dc in next sc, 1 sc in next dc. Rep from * across row. Ch 2, turn. (*Note:* In this pattern, the turning ch-2 does *not* count as the first dc of a row.)
Rep Rows 2 and 3 for pat.

Squares: Make 12 with light blue, 11 with dark blue. Ch 18. Work even in pat st for 14 rows. Fasten off.

Half-squares: Make 6 in light blue and 6 in dark blue. Ch 2.
Row 1: (1 sc, 1 dc, 1 sc) in 2nd ch from hook—3 sts. Ch 1, turn.
Row 2: (1 sc, 1 dc) in first st, 1 sc in next st, (1 dc, 1 sc) in last st—5 sts. Ch 1, turn.
Row 3: (1 sc, 1 dc) in first st, work in pat to last st, (1 dc, 1 sc) in last st—7 sts. Ch 1, turn.
Rep Row 3 until you have completed 10 rows—21 sts. Fasten off.

Quarter-squares: Make 2 in light blue and 2 in dark blue. Follow the instructions for half-squares until you have completed 8 rows—17 sts. Fasten off.

Diamonds: Make 30 in copper, 15 with dark red, and 15 with eggplant. Working in pat st, follow the instructions for the diamond until you have completed 15 rows. Row 15 is an even row with 15 sts. Beginning with Row 16, follow the instructions for decreasing diamonds. Row 28 is the final row, consisting of a 3-st dec. Fasten off.

Blocking: Only the half-squares and quarter-squares need to be blocked before joining. Block the half-squares to triangles 4½ inches on each side with a 7-inch base; block the quarter-squares to 4 inches on each side with a 5-inch base.

Finishing: Follow the placement chart for the positions of the pieces. With wrong sides facing you, sew pieces together. Since pieces are not edged, work into the back vertical loops of side stitches. Don't work too tightly and make sure that the points of the pieces match up.

Border: The pattern stitch requires an uneven number of sts between corner sts. When you work the first round, make sure that each side has an uneven number of stitches. With copper, work 8 rnds of pat st around entire joined piece, working 3 sts in each corner. With dark blue, work 12 more rnds in the same manner and the final rnd in reverse sc. Fasten off.

Blocking: Final blocking is optional. If desired, block to 45 inches by 60 inches.

Tumbling Blocks Afghan—Motif-Placement Diagram

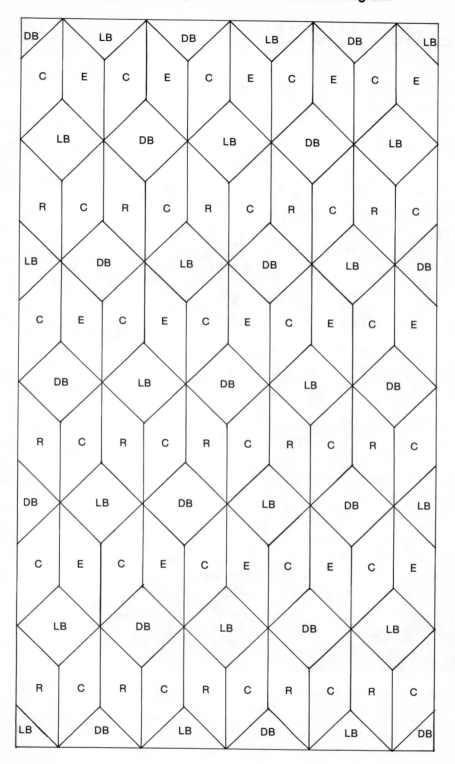

Key
DB = dark blue
LB = light blue
E = eggplant
R = dark red
C = copper

Rectangular Planter

Approximate finished size: Adjustable to fit any container with rectangular sides; as shown, to fit container 3¼ inches by 7¼ inches
No experience needed

This little planter, made of leftover yarn in less than an hour, can be adjusted to cover any container with rectangular sides. Follow the instructions for adjusting the size of a rectangle. Each rectangle should be ¼ inch smaller in both width and length than the side of the container to allow for joining and trim. Work in the main color of each side until you reach the last three rounds and then change colors as given below.

Materials:
Lily 4-ply Sugar 'n' Cream, 70-gram skeins:
 ½ skein color 97, geranium
 ¼ skein color 58, hunter green
 ¼ skein color 62, emerald green
Crochet hook, size F
Container to be covered

Gauge: 2 rounds = 1-inch width

Note: Instructions for working in single-crochet post stitch and for a 3-single-crochet decrease are given in "Terms and Techniques." Instructions for adjusting the size of a rectangle and for working a rectangle are given in "Basic Geometric Shapes."

Rectangles: Make 4. Ch 17. Follow the instructions for the rectangle for 6 rows, changing color as follows:
Rectangle A: Make 2. *Rnds 1 through 3:* geranium; *Rnd 4:* hunter green; *Rnd 5:* emerald green; *Rnd 6:* geranium.
Rectangle B: Make 1. *Rnds 1 through 3:* hunter green; *Rnd 4:* geranium; *Rnd 5:* emerald green; *Rnd 6:* hunter green.
Rectangle C: *Rnds 1–3:* emerald green; *Rnd 4:* hunter green; *Rnd 5:* geranium; *Rnd 6:* emerald green.

Join rectangles: With right sides facing you, join sides with slip stitch through *two back loops only* of opposing pairs of stitches. Use emerald green yarn to join sides of geranium and hunter green and use hunter green to join sides of geranium and emerald green.

Lip: Attach geranium in second st of any rectangle and work 1 rnd of sc post st, working 1 dec in the last st of one rectangle and the first st of the next. Work one more rnd of sc post st, working a 3-sc dec in last st of one rectangle, dec of last rnd, and first st of next rectangle. Fasten off.
Repeat lip on other end.

IV

Stitchery

Textured Squares Afghan

Approximate finished size: Adjustable by size of large 24-inch squares, plus 6 inches for border if desired; as shown, 54 inches on each side. Afghan, as shown, has four large squares.
Average experience necessary

The austere geometry of this white-on-white textural design is created by making and bordering simple single-crochet squares. But this is single crochet with a difference: Instead of working every round in the same direction, the square is turned over at the end of each round. This allows the use of the ridge stitch, an easy and dramatic single-crochet variation that can be worked only back and forth. If turning rounds is new to you, be sure to read the appropriate section in Chapter I before you begin.

Materials:
Reynolds Reynelle, 100-gram skeins:
   13 skeins color 9014, natural
Crochet hook, size G

Gauge: small square = 4 inches square

Note: Instructions for working in turned rounds are given in "To Work in Rounds." Instructions for working in one loop only are given in "Terms and Techniques."

Pattern stitch: Work in sc through the *loop farthest away from you,* *except* at end of rnds join with sl st through *both* loops of first sc.
Small squares: Make 16. Ch 4, join with sl st to make a ring.
Rnd 1: Ch 1, 8 sc in ring—8 sts. Join with sl st to first sc. Ch 1, *turn.*
Rnd 2 (front): 1 sc in first sc, *3 sc in next sc, 1 sc in next sc. Rep from * twice, 3 sc in last sc—3 sts between corner sts. Join with sl st to first sc. Ch 1, *turn.*
Work 5 more rnds in this manner, working 1 sc in every sc and 3 sc in corner sts. Rnd 7 will have 13 sts between corner sts. Fasten off.

Join small motifs: With fronts of two motifs facing you, single crochet through *all four loops* of opposing pairs of stitches; then join two-motif pieces in same manner to make four 4-motif medium squares.

Border the medium squares: With the wrong side of a 4-motif medium square facing you, attach yarn through both loops of any corner st. Work in pattern st, working 3 sts in each corner st, until you have completed 6 rnds. Fasten off. Border remaining three medium squares in same manner.

Join medium squares: Join four medium squares in the same manner that you joined the small squares.

Border large square: Work 6 rounds of border around the large square in the same manner as above. You have completed one large square. For the afghan as shown, make three more large squares.

Join and border afghan: Join four large squares in the same manner as above, and work 14 rounds of border around entire joined piece.

Karate Kid Jacket and Pants

Approximate finished size: Size 2 Toddler (see placement diagram for dimensions in inches)
No experience necessary

The T shape and split sides of the kimono jacket and the adjustable waist of the matching pants help ensure that this outfit won't be outgrown too quickly. If your karate kid is larger than a size 2 Toddler, you can increase the overall size of both jacket and pants by adding one or two rounds of single crochet to each motif or you can add rounds of single crochet to each garment piece (see diagram) before joining the pieces.

Materials:
Berella "4" Yarn by Bernat Yarn and Craft Corporation, 100-gram skeins:
   3 skeins color 8990, violet
   ¼ skein color 8967, marine blue
   ¼ skein color 8933, scarlet
Crochet hooks, sizes H and I
Yarn needle
¾-inch-wide elastic for waistband, if desired

Gauge: 1 motif = 3 inches on each side

Note: Instructions for working in turned rounds, for single-crochet post stitch, and for working in one loop only are given in "Terms and Techniques."

Border pattern stitch: Work with *wrong* side facing you. Attach yarn and ch 1, 1 hdc in first st, *1 sl st in next st, 1 hdc in next st. Rep from * for pat. Stay in pat when working 3 sts in corners.

Squares: Make 88 in violet with I hook. Ch 2.
Rnd 1 (wrong side): In second ch from hook, work (1 sc, 1 dc) 4 times—8 sts. Join with sl st to first sc.
Rnd 2: Ch 1, (1 sc, 1 dc) in every st—16 sts. Join with sl st to first sc. Ch 1, *turn.*
Rnd 3 (front side): Ch 1, 3 sc in first st, *1 sc in each of next 3 sts, 3 sc in next st. Rep from * twice, 1 sc in each of last 3 sts—5 sts between corner sts. Join with sl st to first sc.
Rnd 4: Work in *back loops only.* Ch 1, 1 sc in first st, *3 sc in next st, 1 sc in each of next 5 sts. Rep from * 3 times, ending last rep with 1 sc in each of last 4 sts—7 sts between corner sts. Join to first sc with sl st. Fasten off.

Join motifs: With front sides facing you, join motifs with slip stitch through the *back loops only* of opposing pairs of stitches. Follow the diagram for number and placement of motifs in each piece.

Blocking: Block joined pieces. See diagram for each measurement.

Finishing pants: Fold each half of the pants along the side seam and, working as above, join the first three motifs of each half to each other at center front and center back. Then join the inseam, working from the bottom of one leg around to the bottom of the other.

Waistband: With H hook, attach yarn at center back. Working in *back loop only*, work a row of sc around waist. When you reach center back again, do not join. Instead, ch 1 and turn. Work 4 more rows of sc through *both loops* of sts. *Next Row (wrong side):* Work in sc post st so that the heads of the sts are pushed *away* from you to the front side of the piece. Work 4 more rows of sc. Fasten off. The waistband will naturally fold over at the post st row. Sew the final row to the inside of the pants. Cut elastic to appropriate length and thread it through the waistband. Sew elastic together; then sew center back seam closed. If preferred, the opening can be considered center front and a cord can be threaded through to be tied at front.

Border pants: Work one row of border pattern around the bottom of each leg and into the heads of the sts at waist pushed forward by the post st row.

Finishing jacket: Attach scarlet at side seam of sleeve (see diagram) and work 4 rows of sc from side seam to side seam, working 3 sc in corners. Fasten off.

From now on the front and back trims are worked separately, leaving 5 stitches of scarlet empty at neckline. To keep the front side of the motifs on the front, the right and left sides must be worked in reverse order. Work them in the same way, but begin one with the *front* side facing you and the other with the *wrong* side facing you.

Front: Attach marine blue at side seam. Work in sc as before until you have completed 17 sts on center front, then turn. Work two more rows between side seam and neckline, then two final rows on center front *only* from neckline to corner st.

Back: Work as for front, *but* work 20 sts on center back.

Join top of jacket: With marine blue, join at center back with a slip stitch through *all four loops* of opposing pairs of stitches. With wrong sides facing you, and matching yarn to color of pieces, sew the underarm seams and the side seams together. With front side facing you, work 1 row of single crochet around lower edge of top with violet.

Join top and bottom of jacket: Join the front and back sections of the bottom of the jacket to the top, working as for joining motifs.

Border jacket: Work 1 row of border pattern around sleeves, bottom of jacket, neckline, and center front, changing color to match the border color to the color of the stitches into which you are working.

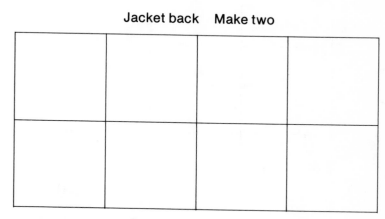

Jacket back   Make two

Sleeve   Make two

cb   side seam   cf

shoulder seam

Jacket Front   Make Two

**Karate Kid Jacket
Motif-Placement Diagram**

cb   cf

1 square = 3 inches = 1 motif

pants   Make two

cf   side seam   cb

Karate Kid Pants
Motif-Placement Diagram

Puffed-Shells Baby Blanket

*Approximate finished size: Adjustable to any multiple of 9 inches plus
4 inches for border*
Average experience needed

A friend of mine discovered the pattern for these marvelously puffed-out shells in a
book of Victorian crochet patterns. Because the five stitches of each shell are never
joined to each other or worked into on subsequent rounds, they are never pulled back
down to the surface of the piece. This creates their sculptured shape. I emphasized
what seemed to me to be their essentially modern look by working in bold primary colors. A more properly Victorian combination might be plum and forest green.

Materials:
Berella "4" Yarn by Bernat Yarn and Craft Corporation, 100-gram skeins:

    4 skeins color 8933, scarlet
    3 skeins color 8967, marine blue
Crochet hook, size I

Gauge: 1 motif = 9 inches on each side

Note: Instructions for working in one loop only, for working over one row into the row below, and for the post stitch are given in "Terms and Techniques."

Puffed-shell stitch: When stitches are worked in the back loops only, the empty front loops form short horizontal bars on the front. To make a puffed shell, do not work in the next stitch, but into the empty front loop of the stitch a row below. On the following round, the 5 double crochets of the shell are left empty, allowing the shell to puff. Instead, a stitch is worked into the empty stitch of the previous row, which is behind the shell. Each puffed shell is composed of 5 double crochets.

Squares: Make 4 with marine blue as main color (MC) and scarlet as trim color (TC), and 12 with scarlet as MC and marine blue as TC. Work in *back loops only* through Rnd 7 but always join with sl st through *both* loops of first st. With MC, ch 2.
Rnd 1: 8 sc in second ch from hook—8 sts. Join to first sc with sl st.
Rnd 2: Ch 1, 1 sc in first st, *3 sc in next st, 1 sc in next st. Rep from * twice, 3 sc in last st—3 sts between corner sts. Join to first sc with sl st.
Rnd 3: Ch 1, 1 sc in each of first 2 sts, *3 sc in corner st, 1 sc in each of next 3 sts. Rep from * 3 times, ending last rep with 1 sc in last st—5 sts between corner sts. Join to first sc with sl st.
Rnd 4: Ch 1, skip first st and work 1 puffed shell into the front loop of the st directly below in Rnd 2. *1 sc in each of next 2 sts, 3 sc in corner, 1 sc in each of next 2 sts, skip next st and work 1 puffed shell into empty front loop of Rnd 2. Rep from * 3 times, ending last rep with 1 sc in each of last 2 sts. Join to first (skipped) st of Rnd 3, which is behind shell.

Rnd 5: Ch 3 (counts as 1 dc), *1 sc in each of next 3 sc, 3 sc in corner, 1 sc in each of next 3 sc, 1 dc in skipped st behind shell. Rep from * 3 times, ending last rep with 1 sc in each of last 3 sc. Join to top of starting ch-3 with sl st.

Rnd 6: Ch 1, 1 sc in each of first 2 sts, *skip next st and work 1 puffed shell into the empty front loop of the st directly below in Rnd 4, 1 sc in each of next 2 sts, 3 sc in corner, 1 sc in each of next 2 sts, skip next st and work 1 puffed shell in front loop of st in Rnd 4, 1 sc in each of next 3 sts. Rep from * 3 times, ending last rep with 1 sc in last st. Join to first st with sl st.

Rnd 7: Ch 1, 1 sc in each of first 2 sts, *1 dc in skipped st behind shell, 1 sc in each of next 3 sts, 3 sc in corner, 1 sc in each of next 3 sts, 1 dc in skipped st behind shell, 1 sc in each of next 3 sts. Rep from * 3 times, ending last rep with 1 sc in last st. Join to first sc with sl st. Ch 1, *turn.*

Rnd 8 (wrong side): Work in loop *farthest away from you,* which is front loop. Work 1 sc in every st, 3 sc in corners—15 sts between corners. Join to first sc with sl st. Ch 1, *turn.*

Rnd 9: Work in *back loops only.* Work 1 sc in every st, 3 sc in corner sts—17 sts between corner sts. Join to first sc with sl st. Fasten off.

Rnd 10: Attach TC around turning ch-1. Ch 2, work dc post st around post of every st, working 3 dc *over* corner st into corner st of Rnd 8—19 sts between corner sts. Skip attaching ch-2 and join to first dc with sl st. Ch 1, *turn.*

Rnd 11: Work in loop *farthest away from you only,* which is the front loop. Work 1 sc in every st, 3 sc in corners—21 sts between corner sts. Join to first sc with sl st. Ch 1, *turn.*

Rnd 12: Work in *back loops only.* Work 1 sc in every sc, 3 sc in corners—23 sts between corner sts. Join to first sc with sl st. Fasten off.

Rnd 13: With front facing you, attach MC around turning ch-1, ch 2. Work 1 dc post st around post of every st, working 3 tr *over* the corner sts of Rnds 12 and 11 and into the corner st of Rnd 10—25 sts between corner sts. Join with sl st to first dc. Fasten off.

Join squares: With marine blue, join the four marine blue squares with a slip stitch through *all four loops* of opposing pairs of stitches. With scarlet, join scarlet squares to make outer round of motifs. Then join the center square of marine blue motifs to the outer round of scarlet motifs with marine blue.

Border: With front side facing you, attach scarlet in any corner. Ch 3 (counts as 1 dc), work one rnd of dc, working 3 dc in corners. Join to first dc with sl st, *turn*.

Rnd 2: Work in loop *farthest away from you only*, which is front loop. Ch 1, work 1 sc in every st, working 3 sc in corners. Join to first sc with sl st. Fasten off.

Rnd 3: With front side facing you, attach marine blue around post of ch-1 turning ch. Ch 2. Work 1 dc post st around every st, working 3 dc post sts around corner st. Join to first dc with sl st. Ch 1, *turn*.

Rnd 4: 1 hdc in first st, *1 sl st in next st, 1 hdc in next st. Rep from *, working 3 sts in corners. Fasten off.

Shell-Stitch Baby Blanket

Approximate finished size: Length adjustable by multiple of 4½ inches; as shown, 30 inches by 40 inches without tassels
Average experience needed

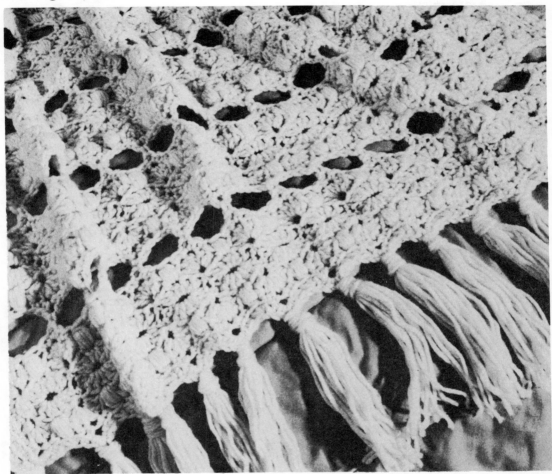

When rectangular motifs are worked in a design that involves fancy stitches, it is difficult to adjust the length or width of a motif. Of course, you need only add more motifs to increase the length. If, however, this combination of texture and openwork appeals to you as an afghan, you can double or triple the width by working one or two more strips of motifs. Join motifs to those of adjacent strips through the corner stitches only and you will create an openwork pattern between strips to complement the pattern between motifs of the same strip.

Materials:
Berella "4" Yarn by Bernat Yarn and Craft Corporation, 100-gram skeins:
  4 skeins color 8940, natural
Crochet hook, size I

Gauge: 1 motif = 4 inches by 28 inches

Note: Instructions for working in one loop only and working over one row into the row below are given in "Terms and Techniques." Instructions for joining as you work are given in "Finishing Techniques."

Pineapple stitch: In next st, (yo and draw up a loop) 4 times, yo and draw through all but 1 loop on hook, yo and draw through last 2 loops.

Motif: Make 9 with natural. Ch 92.
Rnd 1: 1 sc in second ch from hook, *skip 2 ch, 5 dc in next ch (1 shell), skip 2 ch, 1 sc in next ch. Rep from * across ch, ending last rep with 5 sc in last ch. Working on other side of ch, *skip next 2 ch, 1 shell in next ch (same ch holding shell on other side), skip next 2 chs, 1 sc in next ch. Rep from * across ch, ending last rep with 4 sc in ch holding first sc—15 shells on each side of ch. Join to first sc with sl st.
Rnd 2: Ch 3 (counts as 1 dc), 4 dc in *back loop only* of first st, *1 sc through *both loops* of center (3rd) dc of shell, 1 shell in *back loop only* of next sc. Rep from * across side, ending last rep with 1 shell in back loop of first sc of 5-sc corner group, 1 sc in back loop of each of next 3 sc, 1 shell in back loop of next sc. Rep from * across side, ending with 1 shell in first of 5-sc corner group, 1 sc in back loop of each of next 3 sts. Join to top of ch-3 with sl st.
Rnd 3 for first motif: Ch 1, 1 sc in each of first 2 sts, [(2 sc, ch 3, 2 sc) in center dc of first shell, *1 sc in next dc, skip next dc, working over next sc, work 1 pineapple in center st of shell below, skip next dc, 1 sc in next dc, (1 sc, ch 3, 1 sc) in center dc. Rep from * across side, ending with (2 sc, ch 3, 2 sc) in center dc of last shell, 1 sc in each of next 7 sts]. Rep within brackets once, ending with 1 sc in each of last 5 sts. Join with sl st to first sc. Fasten off.

Rnd 3 for subsequent motifs: Work as above but do not rep within brackets. As you work second side, you will join this motif to already completed motif. Work 2 sc in center dc of first shell, ch 1, sl st in ch-3 picot of first shell of completed motif, ch 1, 2 more sc in center st of first shell. Continue to work as for first side *except* in center of each shell, work as follows: 1 sc in center dc of shell, ch 1, 1 sl st in ch-3 picot of opposing shell of completed motif, ch 1, 1 more sc in center dc. End rnd with 2 sc in last shell, ch 1, sl st in ch-3 picot of last shell of completed motif, ch 1, 2 more sc in last shell, 1 sc in each of last 5 sts. Join to first sc with sl st. Fasten off.

Border: Attach yarn in ch-3 corner so that you will first work across top or bottom. Working in *back loop only*, [(2 sc, ch 3, 2 sc) in corner ch-3, 1 sc in each of next 2 sts, *1 3-sc dec in next 3 sts, 1 sc in next st, (2 sc, ch 3, 2 sc) in ch-3 picot, 1 sc in next st. Rep from * across, (2 sc, ch 3, 2 sc) in next ch-3 corner, 1 sc in every st to next corner]. Rep within brackets once. Join with sl st to first sc. Fasten off.

Side border: With *wrong* side facing you, attach yarn in ch-3 corner so that you will be working down side of piece. Work these two rows on sides only.
Row 1: Working in loop closest to you *only*, work 1 hdc in ch-3 corner, *1 sl st in next st, 1 hdc in next st. Rep from * across side. Fasten off.
Row 2: With wrong side facing you, attach yarn in first hdc of Row 1. 1 sl st in first hdc, *1 hdc in next sl st, 1 sl st in next hdc. Rep from * across side. Fasten off. Repeat border on other side.

Blocking: Blocking is optional.

Tassels: For each tassel, wrap yarn around 8-inch piece of cardboard 10 times and cut it at one end. Keeping the cut ends as even as possible, hold the yarn in the center and pull it through the ch-3 picot from back to front. Bring the cut ends up through the loop you have created, and gently pull to close. Put one tassel in ch-3 loop of each shell.

Half-Double-Crochet
Sampler Pillow

*Approximate finished size: Adjustable by multiple of 3½ inches plus
12 inches for border; as shown, 26 inches square*
Average experience necessary

The half-double crochet has always been my favorite stitch. Worked alone or in patterns, it creates some of the most beautiful textures in crochet. Yet it is used much less frequently than the single or double crochet. Perhaps its lack of popularity is due to hiding its best side—the most interesting textures and patterns appear on the *wrong* side of the piece. As you make this pillow, a sampler of half-double-crochet stitch patterns, you'll see what I mean; every round but one is worked so that the pattern comes up on the side facing away from you.

Materials:
Lily 4-ply Sugar 'n' Cream, 70-gram skeins:
   3 skeins color 3, cream
   1 skein color 46, rose pink
   1 skein color 42, tea rose
   1 skein color 26, light blue
Crochet hook, size G
For pillow:
   Two 28½-inch squares of fabric, color-coordinated with yarn
   Sewing thread to match fabric
   Polyester stuffing

Gauge: 1 motif = 3½ inches on each side

Note: Because the pattern comes up on the side facing away from you, the usual designations of front and wrong side are confusing. For this project, "pattern side" and "nonpattern side" will be used. Instructions for working in turned rounds are given in "To Work in Rounds." Instructions for making a pillow are given in "Finishing Techniques."

Pattern stitches:
Daisy stitch: Ch 1, hold ch-1 sp open with thumb and forefinger of left hand, insert hook into it and draw up a loop—2 loops on hook. Draw up a loop in each of first 3 sts—5 loops on hook. Yo and draw through all 5 loops on hook. *Ch 1, insert hook in ch-1 sp and draw up a loop, draw up a loop in same st in which last daisy st was completed and in each of next 2 sts, yo and draw through all 5 loops on hook. Rep from * for pat.
Pattern stitch for border: Work on uneven number of stitches.
Rnd 1: Ch 1, [1 sl st in first st of side, *1 hdc in next st, 1 sl st in next st. Rep from * across side, (1 hdc, ch 2, 1 hdc) in corner st]. Rep within brackets 3 times; join to first sl st with sl st.
Rnd 2: Ch 1, [1 hdc in first st, *1 sl st in next hdc, 1 hdc in next sl st. Rep from *across side, (1 sl st, ch 2, 1 sl st) in corner ch-2]. Rep within brackets 3 times; join to first hdc with sl st.
Rep Rnds 1 and 2 for pat.

Motif: Make 16 with cream. Ch 5, join with a sl st to make a ring.

Rnd 1 (nonpattern side): Ch 1, 12 hdc in ring, join to first hdc with sl st—12 sts.

Rnd 2: Ch 1, (1 hdc, 1 sl st) in each st—24 sts. Join to first hdc with sl st.

Rnd 3: Ch 1, 1 hdc in first st, *skip next st, 7 hdc in next st, skip next st, 1 hdc in each of next 3 sts. Rep from * 3 times, ending last rep with 1 hdc in each of last 2 sts—fourth hdc of 7-hdc group is corner st; 9 sts between corner sts. Join to first hdc with sl st.

Rnd 4: Ch 1, 1 hdc in first st, 1 sl st in next st, 1 hdc in next st, 1 sl st in next st, *(1 hdc, ch 2, 1 hdc) in corner st, (1 sl st in next st, 1 hdc in next st) 4 times, 1 sl st in last st of side. Rep from * 3 times, ending last rep with (1 sl st in next st, 1 hdc in next st) twice, 1 sl st in last st—11 sts between ch-2 corners. Join to first hdc with sl st. Fasten off.

Blocking: Pattern side up, block motifs to 3½ inches on each side.

Join motifs: With nonpattern sides of two motifs facing you, attach yarn in ch-2 corners. Sl st through all four loops of opposing pairs of sts to next ch-2 corners. Fasten off. Repeat to join motifs into four strips of four motifs each; then join strips to make a square.

Border: With nonpattern side facing you, attach cream in any ch-2 corner and work 1 rnd of hdc, working 3 hdc in corners. The next rnd requires an even number of stitches, so make sure that you have an even number on each side between corner sts. Join to first hdc with sl st; *turn.*

Rnd 2: Work one rnd of daisy st, working (1 hdc, ch 2, 1 hdc) in corner sts. Join to first st with sl st; *turn.*

Rnd 3: Ch 1, *1 hdc in first hdc, (1 hdc, ch 2, 1 hdc) in ch-2 corner, 1 hdc in next hdc, 2 hdc in ch-1 sp of each daisy across side, rep from * 3 times. Join to first hdc with sl st.

Rnd 4: (*Note:* The border pat, which begins with the next rnd, requires an uneven number of sts, so that you must dec 1 st each side on this rnd.) Work rnd in hdc, working (1 hdc, ch 2, 1 hdc) in corners, *but* skip first hdc of each side. Fasten off.

Rnds 5–22: Work in border pat, changing yarn as follows: *Rnd 5:* tea rose; *Rnd 6:* light blue; *Rnd 7:* rose pink; *Rnd 8:* tea rose; *Rnd 9:* rose pink; *Rnd 10:* light blue; *Rnd 11:* tea rose; *Rnd 12:* light blue; *Rnd 13:* rose pink; *Rnds 14–17:* cream; *Rnd 18:* tea rose; *Rnds 19–21:* rose pink; *Rnd 22:* tea rose. Fasten off.

Finishing: Block pillow front to 28 inches on each side. Make and stuff a 28-inch square pillow and sew the crocheted pillow front to one side.

Aran Isle Floor Pillow

Approximate finished size: 30 inches on each side
Experience needed

The classic raised designs of Aran Isle patterns appear almost to be carved from the rocky cliffs of the Irish coast from which they come. Crochet cannot produce true cables, but it can beautifully replicate the multistitch, multitexture look of fisherman knits—and in much less time. This pillow is a sampler of crocheted Aran Isle patterns, any of which can be used in sweaters, hats, mittens, or afghans to create the sculptural beauty of Aran Isle designs.

Materials:
Reynolds Highland Worsted, 100-gram skeins:
    6 skeins color 405, ecru
Crochet hook, size F
Yarn needle
For pillow:
    Two 30½-inch squares of fabric, color-coordinated to yarn
    Sewing thread to match fabric
    Polyester stuffing

Gauge: In hdc/sl st pat, 11 stitches = 2 inches; 5 rows = 1 inch

Note: Instructions for working in turned rounds and for the single-crochet post stitch are given in "Terms and Techniques." Instructions for making and stuffing a pillow are given in "Finishing Techniques."

Long treble: Yo twice, insert hook from front to back to front around post of st 2 rnds below and gently draw up a long loop of about ¾ inch; (yo and draw through 2 loops) 3 times to complete treble.

Hazelnut stitch: Work with wrong side facing you. In next st, (yo, draw up a loop, yo, draw through 2 loops) 4 times, yo and draw through all 5 loops on hook, at the same time pushing the hazelnut away from you to the front side.

Long single crochet: Do not work in next st. Instead, insert hook in appropriate st of row below, yo and gently draw up a long loop until it is even with the rest of the sts in the row being worked. Yo and complete the sc.

Cable: Each cable is completed before the next is begun. You must turn your work twice in the process of completing each cable. Notice that after these turns, you *do not* ch up. 1 sc in first st, *ch 4, skip 3 sts, 1 sc in next st, *turn*, 1 sc in each ch, 1 sl st in sc, *turn*; holding the cable toward you, work 1 sc in each of the 3 skipped sts. Rep from * for each of the cable.

Center square: Ch 2.

Row 1: (1 hdc, 1 sl st, 1 hdc) in second ch from hook—3 sts. Ch 1, turn.

Row 2: (1 hdc, 1 sl st) in first hdc, 1 hdc in sl st, (1 sl st, 1 hdc) in last hdc—5 sts. Ch 1, turn.

Row 3: (1 hdc, 1 sl st) in first hdc, *1 hdc in next sl st, 1 sl st in next hdc. Rep from * across row to last st, (1 sl st, 1 hdc) in last st—7 sts. Ch 1, turn. Rep Row 3 for pat until the sides of the piece measure 19 inches and the last row measures 28 inches, approximately 65 rows for 131 sts.

Next row: Yo, draw up a loop through each of first 2 sts, yo and draw through all 4 loops on hook (counts as 1 hdc dec). Work in pat to last 2 sts, 1 hdc dec in last 2 sts. Ch 1, turn.

Repeat this row until 3 sts remain. Work a 3-st dec in last 3 sts. Fasten off.

Blocking: Block center square to 19 inches square.

Rectangular panels: Make 4. Ch 74.

Row 1: 1 sc in second ch from hook and in every ch across row—73 sts. Ch 1, turn.

Rows 2, 3, and 4: Work even in sc—73 sts. Ch 1, turn.

Row 5: 1 sc in each of first 3 sts; working *over* next st, work 1 long tr around post of st directly below in Rnd 2, *skip next 4 sts of Row 2 and work another long tr around post of next st, skip 2 sts of Row 5, 1 sc in each of next 4 sts, 1 long tr around post of st in Row 2 adjacent to that used for last long tr. Rep from * across row, ending with 1 long tr around post of second to last st of Row 2, skip 2 sts of Row 5, 1 sc in each of last 2 sts—73 sts; 12 long tr V's. Ch 1, turn.

Row 6: 1 sc in each of first 5 sts, *1 hazelnut in next st, 1 sc in each of next 5 sts. Rep from * across row, ending with 1 sc in each of last 7 sts—73 sts; 11 hazelnuts. Ch 1, turn.

Rows 7 and 8: 1 sc in every st across row—73 sts. Ch 1, turn.

Row 9: 1 sc in first st, 1 long tr around post of st in Row 6 *directly above* the first long tr of Row 5, skip next st of Row 9, *1 sc in each of next 4 sts of Row 9, 1 long tr around st of Row 6 adjacent to last long tr (directly above next long tr of Row 5), 1 long tr above next long tr of Row 5 (on the other side of hazelnut), skip 2 sts of Row 9. Rep from * across row, ending with 1 long tr above last long tr of Row 5, 1 sc in last st—74 sts. Ch 1, turn.

Row 10: Skip first st, 1 sc in next st and every st across row—73 sts. Ch 1, turn.

Row 10 is the last row worked back and forth. From now on, you will work around the entire panel in rounds.

Rnd 11: 1 sc in each of first 4 sts, *1 long sc over next st into sp in Row 6 between the 2 long trs, 1 sc in each of the next 5 sts. Rep from * across side, ending side with 1 long sc in last sp of Row 6, 1 sc in next st, 3 sc in last st, 9 sc evenly spaced down short side, 3 sc in first ch of foundation ch, 1 sc in each of next 2 ch, *1 long sc in sp directly above long sc of other side, 1 sc in each of next 5 ch. Rep from * across side, ending with 1 long sc in last sp, 1 sc in each of next 2 ch, 3 sc in last ch, 9 sc evenly spaced down short side, 2 sc in same st as first sc of rnd—73 sts on long sides between corner sts; 11 sts on short sides between corner sts. Join with sl st to first sc.

Rnd 12: Ch 1, work 1 sc post st around post of every st, working (1 sc post st, ch 2, 1 sc post st) around corner sts—75 sts and 13 sts between corners. Join with sl st to first sc.

Rnd 13: Ch 1, 1 sc in first st, [*1 cable over next 4 sts. Rep from * across side, ending side with ch 4, skip st holding cable and last st of side, 1 sc in ch-2 corner, turn and work cable, turn and work 1 sc in skipped st, ch 4, 1 sc in first st of short side, turn and work cable, turn and work 1 sc in ch-2 corner, ch 4, skip st holding cable and next 3 sts, 1 sc in next st, turn and work cable. Work 2 more cables on short side. The last of these should end in the last sc of the short side. Ch 4, skip st holding cable, work 1 sc in ch-2 corner, turn and work cable, turn and work 1 more sc in ch-2 corner, ch 4], skip first st of long side, 1 sc in next st, turn and work cable, turn and work 1 sc in skipped st. Rep within brackets, ending with sl st into first sc of rnd, turn and work cable, turn and work 1 sc in skipped st, sl st again into first sc of rnd—18 cables on long sides, 2 cables at corners, 3 cables on short sides.

Rnd 14: [*Skip st holding cable, 2 sc in first of 3 sts under cable, 1 sc in each of next 2 sts. Rep from * to corner cables. 1 sc in st holding first corner cable, 3 sc in ch-2 sp of Rnd 12, skip st holding corner cable on short side, work under short side cables as above, skip st holding corner cable, 3 sc in ch-2 sp, 1 sc under second corner cable.] Rep within brackets—76 sts and 14 sts between corner sts.

Rnd 15: Ch 1, work 1 sc in every st, 3 sc in corners—78 sts and 16 sts between corners. Join to first sc with sl st.

Rnd 16: Ch 1, work 1 sc post st around post of every st, (1 sc post st, ch 2, 1 sc post st) around corner sts—78 sts and 18 sts between corners. Join with sl st to first sc. Fasten off.

Corner squares: Make 4. Ch 4, join to first ch with sl st to make ring.
Rnd 1: Ch 1, 7 sc in ring—7 sts. Join to first sc with sl st.

Rnd 2: Ch 1, 2 sc in every st—14 sts. Join to first sc with sl st. Ch 1, *turn.*

Rnd 3: Ch 1, 1 hazelnut in first st, *2 sc in next st, 1 hazelnut in next st. Rep from * 5 times, 2 sc in last st—21 sts; 7 hazelnuts. Join to first hazelnut with sl st. Ch 1, *turn.*

Rnd 4: 1 sc in each of first 2 sts, *2 sc in hazelnut, 1 sc in each of next 2 sts. Rep from *, ending with 2 sc in last hazelnut—28 sts. Join to first sc with sl st.

Rnd 5: Ch 1, (1 sc post st, ch 2, 1 sc post st) around first st, *1 sc post st around each of next 6 sts, (1 sc post st, ch 2, 1 sc post st) around next st. Rep from * twice, 1 sc post st around each of last 6 sts—8 sts between ch-2 corners. Join to first sc with sl st.

Rnd 6: Ch 1, skip first st, *5 dc in ch-2 sp, skip next st, 1 sc in each of next 6 sts, skip next st. Rep from * 3 times—10 sts between corners. Join to first dc with sl st.

Rnd 7: Ch 1, work 1 sc post st around every st, working (1 sc post st, ch 2, 1 sc post st) around corner sts—12 sts between corners. Join to first sc with sl st.

Rnd 8: Ch 1, work 1 sc in every st, 3 sc in ch-2 corners—14 sts between corners. Join to first sc with sl st.

Rnd 9: Ch 1, rep Rnd 7—16 sts between corners. Join to first sc with sl st.

Rnd 10: Ch 1, rep Rnd 7 *except* work (1 sc, ch 2, 1 sc) in ch-2 corners—18 sts between corners. Join to first sc with sl st. Fasten off.

Join corner squares to rectangles: With front sides facing you, join pieces with sc through *all four loops* of opposing pairs of stitches into square with an empty center.

Join center square to outer square: With wrong sides facing you, sew center square to outer square.

Border: Attach yarn in any ch-2 corner.

Rnds 1 and 2: Ch 1, work 1 sc in every st, 3 sc in ch-2 corners. Join to first sc with sl st.

Rnd 3: Ch 1, work 1 sc post st around every st, (1 sc post st, ch 2, 1 sc post st) in corners. Join to first sc with sl st.

Rnd 4: Ch 1, work as for Rnd 3 *except* work (1 sc, ch 2, 1 sc) in ch-2 corners. Fasten off.

Finishing: Block completed pillow front to 30 inches square. Make and stuff a 30-inch pillow and sew the crocheted piece to one side of it.

Mosaic Baby Blanket

Approximate finished size: 30 inches by 45 inches
Experience needed

The strong pastels and intricate patterns of this mosaic design were selected to bring to mind the multifaceted tile mosaics of the Mediterranean region. Each square is crocheted in the same stitch pattern and color sequence, yet each is unique because the order of the colors varies. A simplified variation, which would eliminate the need to follow the color-placement chart, would be to select one favorite motif—my choice would be Motif 1—and repeat only that motif. A quite different but equally compelling blanket would result.

Materials:

Phildar Luxe 025, 50-gram skeins:

    For mosaic side:

    3 skeins color 64, naiade (aqua)

    2 skeins color 68, nymphette (peach)

    1 skein color 96, violette (lavender)

    1 skein color 03, angelot (light blue)

    1 skein color 69, ondine (dark blue)

    1 skein color 36, feé (light green)

    For backing side:

    6 skeins color 64, naiade (aqua)

Crochet hook, size F

Gauge: 5 rounds = 2¾ inches on each side; mosaic motif = 5¾ inches on each side; joined mosaic and backing motif = 6 inches on each side

Note: Instructions for working over one round into a round below and for reverse single crochet are given in "Terms and Techniques."

Design tip: I wanted this blanket to have warmth and weight but didn't want to sacrifice the thin fingering yarn that made it possible to produce so much interplay of color in each small square. So I backed each motif with a square of solid-color single crochet. Joining the squares back-to-back not only doubled the thickness and created a thermal layer between the two, but had the extra advantage of hiding the wrong side of the mosaic motifs, thus producing a more finished result. However, if you are planning to mount and frame the design, follow the instructions for working the mosaic side only.

Mosaic squares: Make 35. Follow the placement chart for position of colors within each square. With color A, ch 5, join with sl st to first ch to make a ring.

Rnd 1: Ch 1, 12 sc in ring. Change to color B, join to first sc with sl st.

Rnd 2: With color B, ch 3 (counts as 1 dc), 4 dc in first st, *ch 2, skip 2 sts, 5 dc in next st. Rep from * twice, ch 2, skip last 2 sts (third dc of 5-dc group is corner st). Join to top ch of ch-3 with sl st. Fasten off.

Rnd 3: Attach color C in corner dc of any 5-dc group. Ch 1, *3 sc in corner dc, 1 sc in each of next 2 dc; working over ch-2, work 1 sc in each of the 2 empty sc of Rnd 1, 1 sc in each of next 2 dc. Rep from * 3 times. Join to first sc with sl st. Fasten off.

Rnd 4: Attach color D in any corner st. Ch 1, *3 sc in corner st, skip next 3 sts, 3 dc in next st, ch 1, 3 dc in next st, skip next 3 sts. Rep from * 3 times. Join to first sc with sl st. Fasten off.

Rnd 5: Attach color E in first dc to the left of any 3-sc corner group. Ch 1, *1 sc in each of first 3 dc, 1 sc in ch-1 sp, 1 sc in each of next 3 dc, skip next sc; working over corner st, work 5 dc in corner st of Rnd 3, skip next sc. Rep from * 3 times. Join to first sc with sl st. Fasten off.

Rnd 6: Attach color A in corner (third) dc. Ch 1, *3 sc in corner st, 1 sc in each of next 4 sts, skip next st; working over next st, work 3 dc in ch-1 sp of Rnd 4, skip next st, 1 sc in each of next 4 sts. Rep from * 3 times. Join to first sc with sl st. Fasten off.

Rnd 7: Attach color B in sc to left of any corner st. Ch 1, *1 sc in every st to next corner st; working over corner st, work 3 dc in corner st of Rnd 5. Rep from * 3 times. Join to first sc with sl st. Fasten off.

Rnd 8: Attach color C in any corner dc. Ch 1, *3 sc in corner st, (1 sc in each of next 3 sts, skip next st; working over next st, work 3 dc in st directly below in Rnd 6, skip next st) twice, 1 sc in each of last 3 sts of side. Rep from * 3 times. Join to first sc with sl st. Fasten off.

Rnd 9: Attach color F in first st to the left of any 3-sc corner group. Ch 1, *1 sc in each of first 5 sts of side, skip next 2 sts; working over both Rnd 8 and Rnd 7, work 5 dc in center dc of 3-dc group of Rnd 6, skip next 2 sts, 1 sc in each of next 5 sts, skip next st; working over corner st, work (2 dc, ch 2, 2 dc) in corner st of Rnd 7, skip next st. Rep from * 3 times. Join to first st with sl st. Fasten off.

Rnd 10: Attach color E in left outside dc of any (2 dc, ch 2, 2 dc) corner group. Ch 1, *1 sc in each of first 4 sts of this side, skip next st; working over next st, work 3 dc in center dc of 3-dc group in Rnd 8, skip next st, 1 sc in each of next 3 sts, skip next st; working over next st, work 3 dc in center dc of Rnd 8, skip next st, 1 sc in each of next 4 sts, skip next st; working over both ch-2 of Rnd 9 and sc of Rnd 8, work (2 dc, ch 2, 2 dc) in corner st of Rnd 7, skip next dc. Rep from * 3 times. Join to first sc with sl st. Fasten off.

Rnd 11: Attach color D in left outside dc of any (2 dc, ch 2, 2 dc) corner group. Ch 1, *1 sc in each of first 19 sts of this side, skip next dc; working over both the ch-2 sps of Rnds 10 and 9 and the sc of Rnd 8, work 5 dc in the corner st of Rnd 7, skip next st. Rep from * 3 times. Join to first sc with sl st. Fasten off.

Rnd 12: Attach peach in any corner dc. Ch 1, *3 sc in corner st, 1 sc in every st to next corner. Rep from * 3 times—25 sts between corner sts.

Change to aqua on last st. With aqua, join to first st with sl st.

Rnd 13: With aqua, ch 1, 1 sc in first st, *3 sc in corner st, 1 sc in every st to next corner. Rep from * 3 times—27 sts between corner sts. Join to first sc with sl st. If you are planning to make solid backing squares for the mosaic motifs, the motif is now complete. Fasten off. However, if you are planning to work the mosaic side only, work 1 more round of sc with aqua, working 3 sc in corner sts—29 sts between corner sts. Fasten off.

Solid backing squares: Make 35 with aqua. Ch 5, join to first ch with sl st to make a ring.

Rnd 1: 8 sc in ring—8 sts. Join to first sc with sl st.

Rnd 2: Ch 1. Work 1 sc in first st, *3 sc in next st, 1 sc in next st. Rep from * twice, 3 sc in last st—3 sc between corner sts. Join to first sc with sl st.

Rnd 3: Ch 1, 1 sc in each of first 2 sts, *3 sc in corner st, 1 sc in each of next 3 sts. Rep from * 3 times, ending last rep with 1 sc in last st—5 sts between corner sts. Join to first sc with sl st.

Work 10 more rnds in this manner, working 1 sc in every sc and 3 sc in corner sts. Rnd 13 will have 25 sts between corner sts.

Rnd 14: Work in dc, working 3 dc in corner sts—27 sts between corners. Join to first dc with sl st. Fasten off.

Blocking: Block both mosaic and solid squares to 5¾ inches on each side. (If you are working mosaic side only, block to 6 inches on each side.)

Join mosaic and solid motifs: Hold the two pieces together back to back with the fronts facing out and the front of the mosaic motif facing you. With aqua, work 1 round of sc through all four loops of opposing pairs of stitches, working 3 sc in corner sts. Join to first sc with sl st. Fasten off.

Join motifs to each other: Motifs are joined in the same manner whether or not you have backed them. Follow the placement diagram for position of each motif. With fronts facing you, join with single crochet through all four loops of opposing stitches.

Border: Work border rnds in sc, working 3 sc in corner sts. Change color as follows: *Rnds 1 and 2:* aqua; *Rnd 3:* light blue; *Rnd 4:* peach; *Rnd 5:* lavender; *Rnd 6:* light green. With aqua, work a final rnd in reverse sc. Fasten off.

Mosaic Baby Blanket
Motif- and Color Placement Diagram

1	2	3	4	5
6	7	8	9	10
11	12	13	14	15
16	17	18	19	20
21	22	23	24	25
26	27	28	29	30
31	32	33	34	35

Mosaic Baby Blanket
Key to Placement Diagram

	MOTIF 1	MOTIF 2	MOTIF 3	MOTIF 4	MOTIF 5
Color A	aqua	dark blue	aqua	light blue	lavender
Color B	light blue	light blue	light blue	lavender	aqua
Color C	peach	lavender	light green	aqua	light green
Color D	light green	aqua	lavender	light green	dark blue
Color E	lavender	peach	dark blue	peach	light blue
Color F	dark blue	light green	peach	dark blue	peach

	MOTIF 6	MOTIF 7	MOTIF 8	MOTIF 9	MOTIF 10
Color A	dark blue	lavender	peach	light green	light blue
Color B	light green	light blue	light green	light blue	peach
Color C	light blue	aqua	aqua	aqua	light green
Color D	lavender	light green	light blue	*peach	lavender
Color E	peach	dark blue	lavender	dark blue	aqua
Color F	aqua	peach	dark blue	lavender	dark blue

	MOTIF 11	MOTIF 12	MOTIF 13	MOTIF 14	MOTIF 15
Color A	lavender	light blue	dark blue	peach	dark blue
Color B	light blue	light green	light blue	aqua	light green
Color C	dark blue	aqua	lavender	light green	aqua
Color D	aqua	dark blue	light green	lavender	light blue
Color E	light green	peach	aqua	light blue	lavender
Color F	peach	lavender	peach	dark blue	peach

	MOTIF 16	MOTIF 17	MOTIF 18	MOTIF 19	MOTIF 20
Color A	dark blue	light green	light green	light blue	light green
Color B	light blue	dark blue	aqua	dark blue	aqua
Color C	light green	light blue	peach	aqua	lavender
Color D	*peach	aqua	light blue	lavender	dark blue
Color E	aqua	lavender	dark blue	peach	peach
Color F	lavender	peach	lavender	light green	light blue

	MOTIF 21	MOTIF 22	MOTIF 23	MOTIF 24	MOTIF 25
Color A	light blue	peach	light blue	light green	light green
Color B	light green	light blue	light green	peach	light blue
Color C	peach	aqua	lavender	aqua	dark blue
Color D	aqua	light green	aqua	light blue	aqua
Color E	lavender	dark blue	peach	dark blue	lavender
Color F	dark blue	lavender	dark blue	lavender	peach

	MOTIF 26	MOTIF 27	MOTIF 28	MOTIF 29	MOTIF 30
Color A	dark blue	light green	peach	dark blue	peach
Color B	peach	light blue	light blue	aqua	dark blue
Color C	aqua	aqua	aqua	light blue	light blue
Color D	light green	lavender	dark blue	lavender	aqua
Color E	light blue	peach	light green	light green	light green
Color F	lavender	dark blue	lavender	peach	lavender

	MOTIF 31	MOTIF 32	MOTIF 33	MOTIF 34	MOTIF 35
Color A	lavender	lavender	light green	lavender	aqua
Color B	aqua	light green	lavender	light green	light green
Color C	light green	light blue	light blue	light blue	light blue
Color D	light blue	*peach	aqua	aqua	dark blue
Color E	dark blue	aqua	dark blue	peach	lavender
Color F	peach	dark blue	peach	dark blue	peach

*Note: When color D is peach, work Round 11 with color C. This is so that 2 rounds of peach will not be next to each other.

Rainbow Afghan

Approximate finished size: Adjustable by multiple of 12 inches, plus 1 inch for border; as shown, 49 inches square
Experience needed

Everybody loves a rainbow. Perhaps we still secretly believe that we might find a pot of gold at its end. The vivid hues of these rainbow motifs, surrounded by white cloudlike shell stitches, will brighten any room but seem ideally suited to the bold, cheerful look that children adore. Incidentally, an unusual floor pillow can be designed by joining four squares so that the rows of white double crochet all face the center. This creates a broken circle of rainbow colors in the center of the square pillow.

Materials:
Berella "4" Yarn by Bernat Yarn and Craft Corporation, 100-gram skeins:

    5 skeins color 8940, natural
    ½ skein color 8933, scarlet
    ½ skein color 8954, orange
    ½ skein color 8903, canary
    ½ skein color 8989, shannon green
    ½ skein color 8967, marine blue
    1 skein color 8990, violet
Crochet hook, size I
Yarn needle

Gauge: 7 dc = 2 inches; 3 dc rows = 2 inches; 1 motif = 12 inches on each side

Note: Instructions for reverse single crochet and working in one loop only are given in "Terms and Techniques."

Squares: Make 16. Squares are identical *except* for color of Row 18 (see instructions following). With natural, ch 4.

Row 1: 3 dc in fourth ch from hook—4 sts. Ch 3 (counts as 1 dc), turn.

Row 2: 1 dc in first st, (2 dc in next st) twice, 1 dc in top of ch-4—7 sts. Ch 3 (counts as 1 dc), turn.

Row 3: 1 dc in first st, *1 dc in next st, 2 dc in next st. Rep from * twice—11 sts. Ch 3 (counts as 1 dc), turn.

Row 4: Skip first st, 1 dc in next st, *2 dc in next st, 1 dc in each of next 2 sts. Rep from * twice—14 sts. Ch 3 (counts as 1 dc), turn.

Row 5: Skip first st, 1 dc in next st, *2 dc in next st, 1 dc in each of next 3 sts. Rep from * twice—17 sts. Ch 3 (counts as 1 dc), turn.

Row 6: Skip first st, 1 dc in each of next 2 sts, *2 dc in next st, 1 dc in each of next 4 sts. Rep from * twice, ending last rep with 1 dc in each of last 3 sts—20 sts. Fasten off.

Rows 7 to 13 are worked in one direction only, fastening off at the end of each row and attaching new yarn in top ch of ch-3 that begins row. Work in *back loops only.*

Row 7: Attach scarlet in top of starting ch-3. Ch 3 (counts as 1 dc), 1

dc in each of next 2 sts, *2 dc in next st. 1 dc in each of next 5 sts. Rep from * twice, ending last rep with 1 dc in each of last 4 sts—23 sts. Fasten off.

Row 8: Attach orange in top of starting ch-3. Ch 3 (counts as 1 dc), 1 dc in each of next 3 sts, *2 dc in next st, 1 dc in each of next 6 sts. Rep from * twice, ending last rep with 1 dc in each of last 4 sts—26 sts. Fasten off.

Row 9: Attach canary in top of starting ch-3. Ch 3 (counts as 1 dc), 1 dc in each of next 4 sts, *2 dc in next st, 1 dc in each of next 7 sts. Rep from * twice, ending last rep with 1 dc in each of last 4 sts—29 sts. Fasten off.

Row 10: Attach shannon green in top of starting ch-3. Ch 3 (counts as 1 dc), 1 dc in each of next 4 sts, *2 dc in next st, 1 dc in each of next 8 sts. Rep from * twice, ending last rep with 1 dc in each of last 5 sts—32 sts. Fasten off.

Row 11: Attach marine blue in top of starting ch-3. Ch 3 (counts as 1 dc), 1 dc in each of next 4 sts, *2 dc in next st, 1 dc in each of next 9 sts. Rep from * twice, ending last rep with 1 dc in each of last 6 sts—35 sts. Fasten off.

Row 12: Attach violet in top of starting ch-3. Ch 3, (counts as 1 dc), 1 dc in each of next 5 sts, *2 dc in next st, 1 dc in each of next 10 sts. Rep from * twice, ending last rep with 1 dc in each of last 6 sts—38 sts. Fasten off.

Row 13: Attach natural in top of starting ch-3. Ch 1, 1 sc in first st, *skip next st, 5 dc (counts as dc shell) in next st, skip next 2 sts, 1 sc in next st. Rep from * twice, skip next 2 sts, 7 tr (counts as 1 tr shell) in next st, *skip next 2 sts, 1 dc shell in next st, skip next st, 1 sc in next st. Rep from * twice ending last rep with skip next 2 sts, 1 sc in last st. Ch 3 (counts as 1 dc), turn.

Rows 14 to 17 are worked through *both loops* of sts.

Row 14: 2 dc in first st, (1 sc in center st of next dc shell, 1 dc shell in next sc) twice, 1 sc in center st of next dc shell, 1 tr shell in next sc, 1 sc in center of next tr shell, 1 tr shell in next sc, (1 sc in center st of next dc shell, 1 dc shell in next sc) twice, 1 sc in center st of last dc shell, 3 dc in last sc. Ch 1, turn.

Row 15: 1 sc in first st, (1 dc shell in next st, 1 sc in center st of next dc shell) twice, 1 tr shell in next sc, 1 sc in center st of next tr shell, 9 tr in next sc (9-tr shell), 1 sc in center st of next tr shell, 1 tr shell in next sc, (1 sc in center st of next dc shell, 1 dc shell in next sc) twice, 1 sc in top of ch-3. Ch 1, turn.

Row 16: 1 sc in each of first 17 sts, 1 tr shell in next sc, 3 sc in center st of 9-tr shell, 1 tr shell in next sc, 1 sc in each of last 17 sts. Ch 1, turn.

Row 17: 1 sc in each of first 21 sts, (5 tr, ch 2, 5 tr) in center sc of 3-sc group at corner, 1 sc in center st of next tr shell and each of last 20 sts. Fasten off.

Row 18: Color varies. Work 4 motifs with scarlet and 3 each with orange, canary, shannon green, and marine blue. Work in *back loops only*. Attach yarn in first sc of Row 17. Ch 3 (counts as 1 dc), skip first st, 1 dc in every st to corner ch-2. Work 3 dc in corner, 1 dc in every st to end of row—27 sts on each side of corner st. Fasten off.

Row 19: With violet, rep Row 18—28 sts on each side. Fasten off.

Block motifs: Block motifs to 12 inches on each side. Motifs will be distorted until blocking.

Join motifs: Place finished edge (edge with violet outer row) of one motif over unfinished edge of adjacent motif. Overlap just enough to cover unfinished edge. With violet, sew motifs together in the following order, according to the color of Row 18: *Row 1:* scarlet, orange, canary, shannon green. *Row 2:* marine blue, scarlet, orange, canary. *Row 3:* shannon green, marine blue, scarlet, orange. *Row 4:* canary, shannon green, marine blue, scarlet.

Border: Only the two unfinished sides of the completed afghan are bordered. With good side facing you, attach violet in corner. Work dcs in sides of sts on the two unfinished sides, working 3 dc in corner. Try to place the sts as carefully as possible. When you reach the end of the second side, do not turn. Work 1 row of reverse sc around entire piece. Fasten off.

Finishing: Block completed afghan to 49 inches on each side.

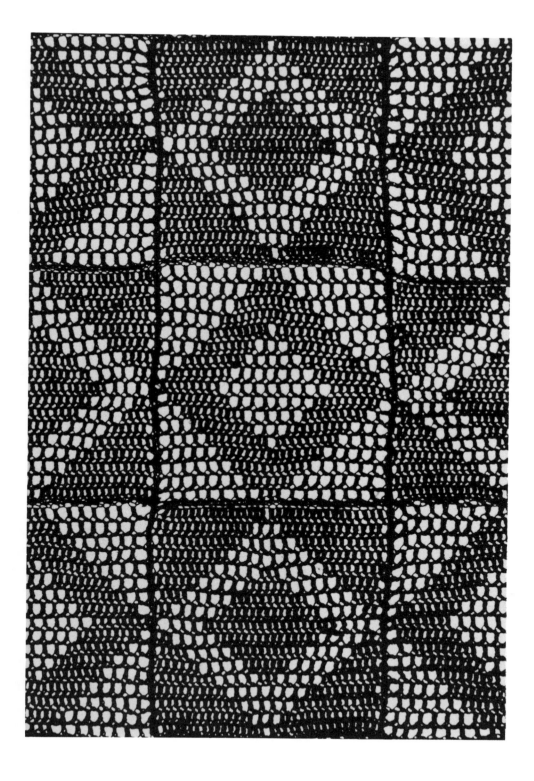

V

Special Crochet

Double-Diamonds Afghan

Approximate finished size: Adjustable by multiple of 11 inches plus 6 inches for border; as shown, 61 inches on each side
Average experience needed

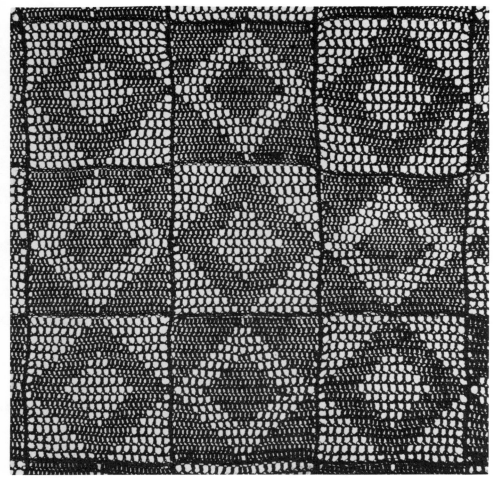

Filet crochet is often considered a time-consuming technique worked with only the tiniest of hooks and thinnest of yarns. Certainly, worked in this traditional manner, it can be used to create unusually realistic "picture lace." But there is no reason to limit this versatile technique to only one style. Modern filet designs, such as this geometric abstract, worked quickly with a large hook in boldly colored worsted-weight yarn, may be better suited to both our tastes and our fast-moving lives. Remember, since filet crochet depends upon solid and open areas to create its effects, it must be displayed against a contrasting background for its drama to be fully appreciated.

Materials:
Brunswick Windrush, 100-gram skeins:
   9 skeins color 9037, raspberry
Crochet hook, size H
Yarn needle

Gauge: 7 stitches = 2 inches; 3 rows = 2 inches; 1 motif = 11 inches
on each side

Note: Instructions for working in filet crochet are given in "Terms and
Techniques."

Square A: Make 13. Follow the graph for placement of open and solid
blocks. Begin as follows: Ch 38.
Row 1: Work 1 dc in sixth ch from hook (counts as 1 dc, ch 1, skip 1
ch), *ch 1, skip 1 ch, 1 dc in next ch. Rep from * 6 times, 1 dc in each
of next 2 chs, *ch 1, skip 1 ch, 1 dc in next ch. Rep from * 7 times;
turn.
Row 2: Ch 4 (counts as 1 dc, ch 1), *skip next ch-1 sp, 1 dc in next dc,
ch 1. Rep from * 5 times, 1 dc in next dc, next ch-1 sp, each of next 3
dc, next ch-1 sp, and next dc. *Ch 1, skip next ch-1 sp, 1 dc in next dc.
Rep from * 6 times, ending last rep with 1 dc in fourth ch of ch-6; turn.
You are now ready to work Row 3 of the chart.

Square B: Make 12. Follow the graph for placement of open and solid
blocks. Begin as follows: Ch 37.
Row 1: 1 dc in fourth ch from hook (counts as 1 dc), 1 dc in each of
next 15 chs, ch 1, skip next ch, 1 dc in each of next 17 chs, turn.
Row 2: Ch 3 (counts as 1 dc), 1 dc in each of next 14 dc, (ch 1, skip 1
st, 1 dc in next st) 3 times, 1 dc in each of last 14 sts, turn.
You are now ready to begin Row 3 of the chart.

Join squares: With wrong sides facing you, sew motifs together, alternating A and B squares as shown in placement diagram.

Border: Work 5 rnds of dc around entire joined piece, working 3 dc in
corners.

Blocking: Blocking is optional.

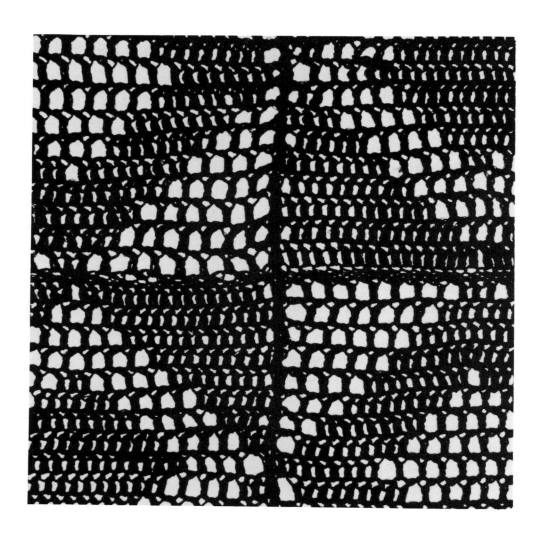

Double-Diamonds Afghan Graph

Motif A: □ = open block
           ⊠ = solid block

Motif B: □ = solid block
           ⊠ = open block

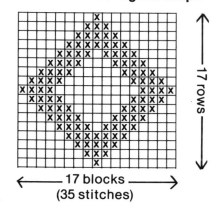

17 rows

← 17 blocks →
(35 stitches)

A	B	A	B	A
B	A	B	A	B
A	B	A	B	A
B	A	B	A	B
A	B	A	B	A

Double Diamonds
Motif-Placement Diagram

Argyle Squares Pillow

*Approximate finished size: Adjustable by multiple of 3¼ inches, plus
6 inches for border*
Average experience needed

The basic square needn't be limited to a single color only. Here a simple tapestry-stitch design and a few rows of weaving combine to produce an apparently complicated argyle pattern. This design, worked with a larger hook to produce a softer fabric, would make a striking front for a sweater, and I think you'll find it easier to work than a knitted argyle design.

Materials:
Phildar Luxe 025, 50-gram skeins:
   1 skein color 11, bois de rose (dusty rose)
   1 skein color 29, bruyère (plum)
   ½ skein color 03, angelot (light blue)
   ½ skein color 71, océan (dark blue)
Steel crochet hook, size 0
Yarn needle
For pillow:
   Two 20½-inch pieces of fabric, color-coordinated with yarn
   Sewing thread to match fabric
   Polyester stuffing

Gauge: 4 rounds = 1¼ inches; 1 square = 3¼ inches on each side

Note: Instructions for working in tapestry stitch are given in "Terms and Techniques." Instructions for the basic square are given in "Basic Geometric Shapes." Instructions for making and stuffing a pillow are given in "Finishing Techniques."

Squares: Make 16. Follow the instructions for the basic square, changing color as given below. With plum, ch 2.
Rnd 1: In second ch from hook, work (1 plum, 1 dusty rose) twice—4 sts. Change to plum on last st; join to first sc with sl st, using plum.
Rnd 2: Ch 1, (3 plum in plum st, 3 dusty rose in dusty rose st) twice—12 sts. Change to plum on last st; with plum, join with sl st to first st.
Rnd 3: Ch 1, 1 plum in first plum, *3 plum in corner st, 1 plum in next plum st, 1 dusty rose in next dusty rose st, 3 dusty rose in corner st, 1 dusty rose in next dusty rose st, 1 plum in next plum st. Rep from * once, ending with 1 dusty rose in last st—4 sts between corner sts. Change to plum on last st; with plum, join to first sc with sl st.
Rnds 4–9: Continue to work plum sts into plum sts and dusty rose sts into dusty rose sts, while you follow the instructions for the basic square. At the end of Rnd 9, *do not* change color. Join and ch 1 with plum.
Rnd 10: On this rnd, colors are reversed. Work dusty rose into plum sts and plum into dusty rose sts—18 sts between corners. Fasten off.

Blocking: Block each square to 3¼ inches.

Join squares: With fronts facing you, sew the squares together through the two back loops of opposing sets of sts. *Note:* This produces a rather wide raised seam. If you prefer a less visible seam, join through the same loops, but with the wrong sides facing you.

Weaving: As you look at the joined squares, you'll see that the 3-sc corner groups produce small spaces that form diagonals across the fabric. You will weave in and out of these spaces, alternating rows of light blue and dark blue (see photograph). For each row of weaving, thread yarn needle with two strands of yarn 48 inches long so that you will be weaving four strands of 24 inches across the rows. If you would like a bulkier, stronger pattern, add a third strand. Begin each row by coming up through the first space and down through the next. Continue across in this manner, working under the center ring of each motif and under the joins between motifs. After you have completed a row of weaving, cut the yarn as close to the needle as possible and tug on the fabric gently to keep it from becoming distorted. Don't knot the yarn tails at either end, but leave about 2 inches of yarn at each end on the wrong side of the pillow. The tails will be hidden between the pillow form and the piece of crochet.

Border: Work rnds of sc around the entire joined piece, working 3 sc in corners. Work 7 rnds with light blue and 12 more rnds with dark blue. Fasten off.

Finishing: If necessary, block completed pillow front to 20 inches square. Make and stuff a 20-inch pillow and sew the crocheted piece to one side of it.

Pinwheel Floor Pillow

Approximate finished size: Adjustable to any multiple of 6½ inches plus 4½ inches for border; as shown, 24 inches on each side
Average experience needed

The light weight of this yarn and the fact that it is machine-washable and dryable make it an excellent choice for baby blankets and crib blankets. If you're looking for such a project, this one can be easily adjusted by adding more Four-Patch and Pinwheel motifs before you add the border. Then, instead of evening out the border with three rounds of single crochet, add just one round, working a chain-4 picot in the point of each shell. If you enjoy working in tapestry stitch, consider making a pillow or blanket using only the Pinwheel motif. The extra effort would be well worth the result.

Materials:
Phildar Luxe 025, 50-gram skeins:
   2 skeins color 71, océan (dark blue)
   1 skein color 69, ondine (medium blue)
   1 skein color 03, angelot (light blue)
   1 skein color 96, violette (lavender)
Crochet hooks, size F for pinwheel motifs, G or H for squares and
   border
Yarn needle
For pillow:
   Two 20½-inch squares of fabric, color-coordinated to yarn
   Sewing thread to match fabric
   Polyester stuffing

Gauge: 1 basic square = 3¼ inches on each side; pinwheel square = 6½ inches on each side

Note: Instructions for working in tapestry stitch and for working a 3-sc dec are given in "Terms and Techniques." Instructions for making a circle and a basic square are given in "Basic Geometric Shapes."

To adjust border: If you adjust the size of the pillow, the border will need adjustment as well. Make sure that the number of sts between corner sts of the rnd preceding the first shell rnd is a multiple of 8 sts plus 5. Work rnds in sc until you reach the correct number.

Pinwheel motifs: Make 5. Rnds 1 through 10 are worked in tapestry st. Since sc is the only stitch used, these instructions will give only the color changes. With dark blue and F hook, ch 2.
Rnd 1: Work 8 dark blue in second ch from hook—8 sts. Join to first st with sl st.
Rnd 2: (1 dark blue, 1 lavender) in each st—16 sts. Change to dark blue on last st. With dark blue, join to first sc with sl st.
Rnd 3: Ch 1, 2 dark blue in first st, *1 lavender in next st, 2 dark blue in next st. Rep from * 6 times, 1 lavender in last st—24 sts. Change to dark blue on last st. With dark blue, join to first st with sl st.
Rnd 4: Ch 1, 2 dark blue in first st, *1 dark blue in next st, 1 lavender in next st, 2 dark blue in next st. Rep from * 7 times, ending last rep

with 1 lavender in last st—32 sts. Change to dark blue on last st. With dark blue, join to first st with sl st.

Rnd 5: Ch 1, 2 dark blue in first st, *1 dark blue in each of next 2 sts, 1 lavender in next st, 2 dark blue in next st. Rep from * 7 times, ending last rep with 1 lavender in last st—40 sts. Change to dark blue on last st. With dark blue, join to first st with sl st.

Rnd 6: Ch 1, 2 dark blue in first st, *1 dark blue in each of next 3 sts, 1 lavender in next st, 2 dark blue in next st. Rep from * 7 times, ending last rep with 1 lavender in last st—48 sts. Join to first st with sl st.

Rnd 7: Ch 1, 2 lavender in first st, *1 dark blue in each of next 4 sts, 1 lavender in next st, 2 lavender in next st. Rep from * 7 times, ending last rep with 1 lavender in last st—56 sts. Join to first st with sl st.

Rnd 8: Ch 1, 2 lavender in first st, *1 lavender in each of next 2 sts, 1 dark blue in each of next 3 sts, 1 lavender in next st, 2 lavender in next st. Rep from * 7 times, ending last rep with 1 lavender in last st—64 sts. Join to first st with sl st.

Rnd 9: Ch 1, 2 lavender in first st, *1 lavender in each of next 4 sts, 1 dark blue in each of next 2 sts, 1 lavender in next st, 2 lavender in next st. Rep from * 7 times, ending last rep with 1 lavender in last st—72 sts. Join to first st with sl st.

Rnd 10: Ch 1, 2 lavender in first st, *1 lavender in each of next 6 sts, 1 dark blue in next st, 1 lavender in next st, 2 lavender in next st. Rep from * 7 times, ending last rep with 1 lavender in last st—80 sts. Change to dark blue on last st. With dark blue, join to first st with sl st. Fasten off lavender.

Rnd 11: Ch 1, work round in dark blue, continuing to follow inc pat for circle—88 sts. Change to light blue on last st. With light blue, join to first st with sl st.

Rnd 12: Ch 1, work round in light blue, continuing to follow inc pat for circle—96 sts. Change to medium blue on last st. With medium blue, join to first st with sl st.

Rnd 13: On this round, the circle is changed into a square. With medium blue, ch 1, 1 sc in each of first 2 sts, *skip next 3 sts, 9 tr in next st, skip next 3 sts, 1 sc in each of next 17 sts. Rep from * 3 times, ending last rep with 1 sc in each of last 15 sts—25 sts between corner sts (fifth tr of 9-tr group is corner st). Join to first st with sl st.

Rnd 14: Ch 1, work 1 sc in every st, 3 sc in corners—27 sts between corner sts. Change to dark blue on last st. With dark blue, join to first st with sl st.

Rnds 15 and 16: With dark blue, rep Rnd 14—31 sts between corner sts after Rnd 16. Fasten off.

Squares: Make 8 with dark blue and 8 with lavender. Two of these squares must fit on one side of the pinwheel square; adjust your hook size to get necessary gauge. Follow the instructions for the basic square for 8 rnds. There will be 14 sts on each side between corners.

Blocking: Block the pinwheel squares to 6½ inches on each side and the basic squares to 3¼ inches on each side.

Join motifs: Follow the placement diagram for the positions of the pinwheel squares and basic squares. With the wrong sides facing you, sew the motifs together through the *two back loops only* of opposing pairs of stitches.

Border: Make sure you have the correct number of sts between corner sts as you work the first 3 rnds so that the shell pat of Rnd 4 will fit. With dark blue, work one row of sc around entire joined piece, working 3 sc in corners—97 sts between corners. With light blue, work 2 more rnds of sc, working 3 sc in corners—101 sts between corner sts after Rnd 3.

Rnd 4: Attach medium blue in any corner. Ch 4 (counts as 1 tr), 12 tr in corner st, skip 2 sts, [*1 sc in next st, skip 3 sts, 7 tr (counts as 1 shell) in next st, skip 3 sts. Rep from * 11 times, 1 sc in next st, skip next 2 sts, 13 tr in corner st, skip next 2 sts]. Rep. within brackets twice, then rep from * 11 times, 1 sc in next st, skip last 2 sts—12 shells on each side; seventh tr of 13-tr corner shell is corner st. Join to top of ch-4 with sl st.

Rnd 5: Ch 1, skip first tr, [1 sc in each of next 5 tr, 3 sc in corner tr, 1 sc in each of next 5 tr, one 3-sc dec in last tr, sc, and first tr of next shell, *1 sc in each of next 2 tr, 3 sc in center tr of shell, 1 sc in each of next 2 tr, one 3-sc dec in next tr, sc, and first tr of next shell. Rep from * 11 times]. Rep within brackets 3 times. Join to first sc with sl st. Fasten off.

Rnd 6: Attach dark blue in any corner. Work [3 sc in corner st, 1 sc in each of next 3 sts, skip next 3 sts, *1 shell in 3-sc dec, skip next 3 sts, 1 sc in center st of 3-sc group, skip next 3 sts. Rep from * 12 times, 1 sc in each of next 3 sts of corner shell]. Rep within brackets 3 times—13 shells on each side. Join to first sc with sl st.

Rnds 7–9: With dark blue, work 2 rnds of sc, working 3 sc in corners. Change to light blue and work 1 more rnd. Fasten off.

Finishing: Block completed pillow front, if necessary, to 24 inches on each side. Make and stuff a 24-inch square pillow, and sew the pillow front to one side of it.

**Pinwheel Floor Pillow
Motif-Placement Diagram**

Key
L = lavender basic square
DB = dark blue basic square
Pinwheel = pinwheel motif

Fiesta Placemats

Approximate finished size: Adjustable by size of placemat; as shown,
12 inches by 16 inches
No experience needed

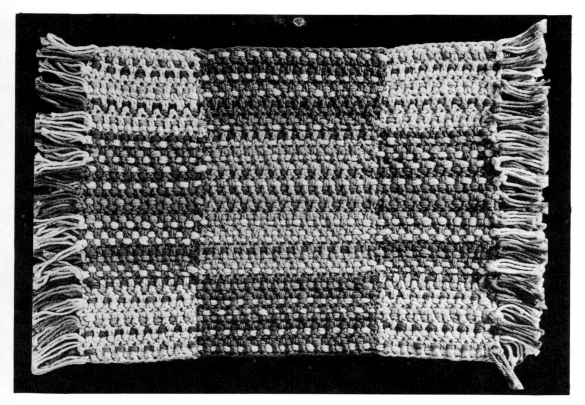

Woven crochet is an easy way to sprinkle a design with color. It is simply what its name implies: First a piece of fabric is crocheted; then yarn is woven through it. Since every strand of woven yarn leaves a yarn tail at each end of the piece, it's a good idea to save heavily woven designs for projects that work well with fringe, such as afghans, shawls, rugs, or these brightly folkloric placemats.

Materials:
Lily 4-ply Sugar 'n' Cream, 70-gram skeins:
  For one placemat:
  1 skein color 28, delft blue
  1 skein color 58, hunter green
  1 skein color 62, emerald green
  Less than ½ skein color 21, shrimp
  Less than ½ skein color 97, geranium
Crochet hook, size G
Yarn needle

Gauge: Before weaving, 7 stitches = 2 inches; 4 rows = 3 inches

Side rectangles: Make 2. With hunter green, ch 18.
Row 1: 1 dc in fourth ch from hook and in every ch across row—16 dc. Ch 3 (counts as 1 dc), turn.
Row 2: Skip first st, 1 dc in every dc across row, ending with 1 dc in top ch of ch-3—16 dc. Ch 3, turn. Rep Row 2 for pat. Work 3 more rows with hunter green, 9 rows with emerald green, and 5 more rows with hunter green. At the end of Row 19, fasten off.

Center rectangle: With emerald green, ch 27. Work as above—25 sts each row. Work 5 rows with emerald green, 9 rows with delft blue, and 5 more rows with emerald green. At the end of Row 19, fasten off.

Join rectangles: With wrong sides facing you, sew pieces together, working in the vertical posts of the opposing stitches.

Weave yarn across placemat: Weaving is done over and under the posts of the double crochets. Each of the 19 rows of double crochet will hold 2 rows of weaving. Begin weaving Row A, working *over* the first double crochet of a row, under the second, and over the third. Begin weaving Row B, working *under* the first double crochet, over the second, and under the third. For each weaving row, thread the yarn needle with two strands of yarn about 52 inches long so that you will be weaving four strands of 26 inches through the piece. Try to keep the four tails as even as possible so that you won't lose a lot of yarn when you trim them. Work in the color order given below. After

121

you have woven the yarn across a row, cut the yarn as close to the needle as possible and tug on the fabric to keep it from bunching.

Color placement for woven rows: *Row 1:* A—hunter green; B—emerald green. *Row 2:* A—geranium; B—shrimp. *Row 3:* A—delft blue; B—hunter green. *Row 4:* A—geranium; B—emerald green. *Row 5:* A—delft blue; B—shrimp. *Row 6:* A—geranium; B—hunter green. *Row 7:* A—delft blue; B—shrimp. *Row 8:* A—hunter green; B—geranium. *Row 9:* A—hunter green; B—emerald green. *Row 10:* A—delft blue; B—emerald green. *Row 11:* A—delft blue; B—hunter green. *Row 12:* A—shrimp; B—hunter green. *Row 13:* A—geranium; B—delft blue. *Row 14:* A—hunter green; B—shrimp. *Row 15:* A—geranium; B—delft blue. *Row 16:* A—emerald green; B—shrimp. *Row 17:* A—hunter green; B—delft blue. *Row 18:* A—geranium; B—shrimp. *Row 19:* A—emerald green; B—hunter green.

Finishing: When the weaving is completed, tug on the piece to loosen the weaving. Loosely knot two yarn tails of a weaving row to the two other tails of that row close to the side of the piece; then trim fringe.

Reverse-Field Placemats

*Approximate finished size: Adjustable by multiple of 3½ inches plus 2
inches for border; as shown, 12½ inches by 16 inches*
Average experience needed

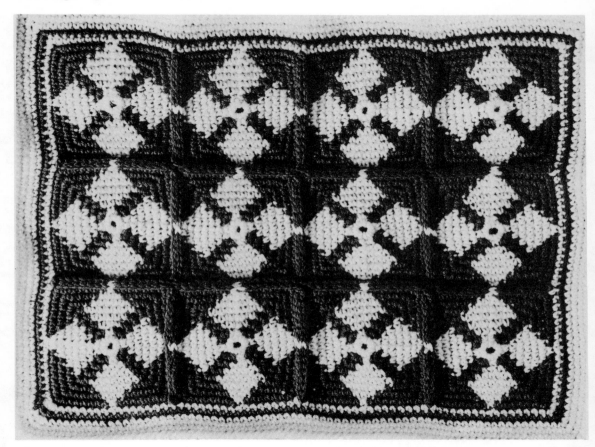

It's remarkable how this design changes when its colors are reversed. Some people
see the dark color as the natural background; others see it as just the opposite. The
colors you choose will strongly affect the design. I chose white and berry for a bright
country look. A dramatic modern combination might be black and a vivid color such
as teal or magenta. Or try a more subtle but still striking set of complementary pastel
colors, such as pale blue and pale peach.

Materials:
Coats and Clark Red Heart Super Sport Yarn, 85-gram skeins:
    For two placemats in reverse colors:
    2 skeins color 744, berry
    2 skeins color 109, ecru
Crochet hook, size F

Gauge: 3 rounds = 1½ inches on each side; 1 square = 3½ inches on each side

Note: Instructions for working in tapestry stitch and for reverse single crochet are given in "Terms and Techniques." Since single crochet is the only stitch used, these instructions will give only the color changes. Color A is the background color, color B is the color of the figure and the trim.

Squares: Make 12 for each placemat. With color A, ch 4, join to first ch with sl st to make a ring.
Rnd 1: Ch 1. With A, work 8 sc in ring—8 sts. Join to first sc with sl st.
Rnd 2: Ch 1, 1 A in first st, *3 B in next st, 1 A in next st. Rep from * twice, 3 B in last st, change to A on last st—3 sts between corner sts. Join to first st with sl st.
Rnd 3: Ch 1, 1 A in each of first 2 sts, *3 B in corner st, 1 A in each of next 3 sts. Rep from * 3 times, ending last rep with 1 A in last st—5 sts between corner sts. Join to first st with sl st.
Rnd 4: Ch 1, 1 A in each of first 3 sts, *3 B in corner st, 1 A in each of next 5 sts. Rep from * 3 times, ending last rep with 1 A in each of last 2 sts—7 sts between corner sts. Join to first st with sl st.
Rnd 5: Ch 1, 1 A in each of first 4 sts, *3 B in corner st, 1 A in each of next 7 sts. Rep from * 3 times, ending last rep with 1 A in each of last 3 sts—9 sts between corners. Join to first st with sl st.
Rnd 6: Ch 1, 1 A in each of first 3 sts, *1 B in each of next 2 sts, 3 B in corner, 1 B in each of next 2 sts, 1 A in each of next 5 sts. Rep from * 3 times, ending last rep with 1 A in each of last 2 sts—11 sts between corner sts. Join to first sc with sl st.
Rnd 7: Ch 1, 1 A in each of first 2 sts, *1 B in each of next 4 sts, 3 B in corner, 1 B in each of next 4 sts, 1 A in each of next 3 sts. Rep from * 3

times, ending last rep with 1 A in last st—13 sts between corner sts. Join to first sc with sl st.

Rnd 8: Ch 1, 1 A in first st, *1 B in each of next 6 sts, 3 B in corner, 1 B in each of next 6 sts, 1 A in next st. Rep from * 3 times, ending last rep with 1 B in last 7 sts, change to A on last st—15 sts between corner sts. With A, join to first sc with sl st. Fasten off.

Join squares: With front sides facing you and with color B, join with sl st through all four loops of opposing pairs of sts. Join squares into three strips of four motifs; then join strips in the same manner.

Border: Work rounds of sc around entire joined piece, working 3 sc in corners. Change color as follows: *Rnd 1:* color A; *Rnd 2:* color B; *Rnds 3–6:* color A. *Rnd 7:* With color A, work final round of reverse sc. Fasten off.

Blocking: Block completed placemat to 12½ inches by 16 inches.

VI

Openwork

Antique Medallion
Placemats and Centerpiece

Approximate finished size: Placemats adjustable by multiple of 4 inches plus 1½ inches for border; centerpiece adjustable by multiple of 5½ inches plus 2½ inches for border
Average experience needed

These classic lace-crochet designs will add Old World elegance and grace to your table for less than two dollars apiece and will require much less work than you might imagine. The motifs worked with the larger hook and yarn, used here for the centerpiece, particularly go quickly. A table runner worked in these large motifs would make a spectacular and inexpensive present. Try working these designs in bright red or turquoise or even black instead of the traditional ecru for a dramatically different effect.

Materials:
J. & P. Coats Knit-Cro-Sheen and Speed-Cro-Sheen:
   For one placemat: 1 ball Knit-Cro-Sheen, in ecru
   For centerpiece: 1 ball Speed-Cro-Sheen, in ecru
Crochet hooks, size F and steel size 1

Gauge: Placemat motif = 4-inch diameter; centerpiece motif = 5½-inch diameter

Note: Instructions for the single-crochet post stitch are given in "Terms and Techniques." Instructions for joining as you work are given in "Finishing Techniques."

Placemat: Make 12 motifs with Knit-Cro-Sheen and steel size 1 hook.
First motif: Ch 8, join to first ch with sl st to make ring.
Rnd 1: Ch 3 (counts as 1 dc), 23 dc in ring—24 sts. Join to top of ch-3 with sl st.
Rnd 2: 1 sc in first st, *ch 14, sl st in third ch from bottom (eleventh ch from hook), ch 2, skip 2 sts, 1 sc in next st. Rep from * 7 times, ending last rep with sl st into first sc of rnd—8 ch-11 loops.
Rnd 3: Sl st into first loop; ch 1. Work (13 sc, ch 2, 13 sc) in every loop. Join to first sc with sl st. Fasten off.

Subsequent motifs: When joining to one other motif, work as above until two empty loops remain in Rnd 3. In next loop, work *13 sc, ch 1, sl st into ch-2 picot of opposing motif, ch 1, 13 more sc in loop. Rep from * in last loop. Join to first sc with sl st. Fasten off. When joining to two other motifs, work Rnd 3 until four empty loops remain. Join next two loops to motif at right and last two loops to motif above that being completed. Work 3 rows of four motifs each.

Fills: Make 6, one in each space between four motifs. Ch 14; join to first ch with sl st to make ring.
Rnd 1: Ch 1, *8 sc in ring, ch 1, sl st around join between two motifs, ch 1. Rep from * 3 times. Join to first sc with sl st. Fasten off.

Half-fills: Make 10, one in each space between two motifs on outside of piece. Ch 14, join with sl st to first ch to make ring.

Rnd 1: Ch 1, sl st into ch-2 picot of right-hand motif, ch 1, 8 sc in ring, ch 1, sl st around join between two motifs, ch 1, 8 sc in ring, ch 1, sl st into ch-2 picot of left-hand motif, ch 1, sl st into ring. Fasten off.

Border: Attach yarn in ch-2 picot of left-hand loop at any corner.
Rnd 1: Ch 13, sl st into ch-2 picot of next corner loop, [*ch 13, sl st around join between motif and half-fill, 8 sc into ring of half-fill, sl st around join between half-fill and next motif. Rep from * until you reach the next corner motif. (Ch 13, sl st into next ch-2 picot of corner motif) twice]. Rep within brackets twice, then rep from * on last side, ending with ch 13, sl st into first ch-2 picot of first corner.
Rnd 2: Sl st into ch-13 corner loop, ch 3 (counts as 1 dc), 6 dc in corner loop, ch 3, 7 more dc in same loop, [*14 dc in next ch-13 loop, 1 dc in each of next 8 sc. Rep from * across side, ending with 13 dc in ch-13 loop before corner loop, (7 dc, ch 3, 7 dc) in corner loop]. Rep within brackets twice, then rep from * on last side, ending with 14 dc in last ch-13 loop. Join with sl st to top of ch-3.
Rnd 3: Ch 1, work 1 rnd in sc, working (2 sc, ch 2, 2 sc) in ch-3 corners.
Rnds 4–5: Work 2 rnds in sc post st, working (1 sc, ch 2, 1 sc) in ch-2 corners. Fasten off.

Blocking: The undulating border is produced by blocking. Instead of pinning the sides into straight lines, pin the corners and then gently stretch the ch-13 loops into curves. Put a few pins inside each curve to hold it in place; then block as usual. The curves will stay until the placemats are washed. After washing and while placemats are still damp, reshape, pinning if necessary, steam lightly, and allow to dry completely in place.

Centerpiece: With F hook and Speed-Cro-Sheen, work as for placemat except make four motifs, one fill, and four half-fills.

Snowflakes Afghan

Approximate finished size: 54 inches square
Average experience needed

Traditionally, motifs have been used to trim all kinds of clothing and home furnishings. Victorian crocheters added motif trims to linens and undergarments, bedspreads and tablecloths, even sheets and towels. So, although I chose to crochet the large center square of the cozy afghan, any fabric of the correct weight and size could be used. When adding motifs to a non-crocheted fabric, you can either sew them on or make a single-crochet border with the correct number of stitches per side (in this case, 131 stitches between corners), sew it to the center square, and crochet the motifs to it.

Materials:
Reynolds Highland Heather, 75-gram skeins:
  14 skeins color 414, blue heather
Crochet hook, size H

Gauge: In center square pattern stitch: 7 stitches = 2 inches; 6 rows = 2 inches

Note: Instructions for joining as you work are given in "Finishing Techniques." Instructions for working in one loop only and for working over one row into the row below are given in "Terms and Techniques."

Design tip: When you join the motifs to the center square, you will need to have exactly 129 stitches between every 3-single-crochet corner group, to give 131 stitches between corners on each side. Unless your piece is 129 rows long, you will not be able simply to work a stitch in the side of each row but will need to adjust the number of stitches per side as you work. A simple way to accomplish this is to divide the side into four equal parts and put markers after each part. You should have made 33 stitches at the first marker, 65 stitches at the halfway point, 97 at the third marker, and 129 in the stitch before the corner stitch. If you count as you go, you'll be able to make any necessary adjustments within each section.

Pineapple stitch: In next st, (yo and draw up a loop) 4 times, yo and draw through all but one loop on hook, yo and draw through last two loops on hook.

Center square: Ch 132.
Row 1: Work 1 sc in second ch from hook, *1 dc in next ch, 1 sc in next ch. Rep from * across chain—131 sts, beginning and ending with sc. Ch 2; turn.
Row 2: Work 1 dc in first sc, *1 sc in next dc, 1 dc in next sc. Rep from * across row—131 sts. Ch 1; turn.
Row 3: Work 1 sc in first dc, *1 dc in next sc, 1 sc in next dc. Rep from * across row—131 sts. Ch 2; turn.
Rep Rows 2 and 3 for pattern. Work even in pattern until the length of the square equals the width, approximately 116 rows. Fasten off.

Border center square: The side you have facing you when you add the border rnd will become the front side of the piece. Attach yarn in first ch of foundation ch. Work 3 sc in corner, 1 sc in each ch of foundation ch to last ch, 3 sc in last ch, work 129 sts evenly spaced in the sides of sts to first st of top row, 3 sc in first st, 1 sc in every st of top row to last st, 3 sc in last st, 129 sts evenly spaced on last side—131 sts between corner sts on each side. Fasten off.

Motifs: Make 40, joining motifs into four 9-motif strips as you work and then adding four corner motifs.

First motif: Ch 2.
Rnd 1: 8 sc in second ch from hook—8 sts. Join to first sc with sl st.
Rnd 2: Ch 1, 1 sc in first st, *ch 5, 1 sc in next st. Rep from * 6 times, ch 2, 1 dc in first sc—8 ch-5 loops.
Rnd 3: *Ch 5, 1 sl st into next ch-5 loop. Rep from * 7 times, ending last rep with sl st in top of dc—8 loops.
Rnd 4: (3 sc, ch 3, 3 sc) in every loop. Join to first sc with sl st. Fasten off.

Subsequent motifs: Work as for first motif until two empty loops remain in Rnd 4. Work *3 sc in next empty loop, ch 1, sl st into ch-3 picot of completed motif, ch 1, 3 more sc in same loop. Rep from * to join last loop to opposing loop of completed motif. Join to first sc with sl st. Fasten off. As you work, make sure there are two empty loops at the top and bottom of each joined motif.

Corner motifs: Each of the four corner motifs joins two 9-motif strips on an angle so that a corner results. Work Rnd 4 of the corner motif until 5 loops remain empty. In next loop, work 3 sc, ch 5, sl st into ch-3 picot of lower side loop of right-hand motif, work 1 sl st in each ch of ch-5, 3 more sc in same loop of corner motif. Join next loop of corner motif to next side loop of right-hand motif, as you have been doing. In next loop of corner motif, work (3 sc, ch 3, 3 sc). Join the last two loops to the side loops of the left-hand motif as for right side. Join to first sc with sl st. Fasten off. The corner motif will have one empty loop at the top and 3 empty loops at the bottom.

Join motifs to square: With the fronts of both the center square and the motifs facing you, attach yarn in any corner st of center square. Ch 1, insert hook through *both* the corner st of square *and* the ch-3 picot at the top of the corner motif and draw up a loop, yo and complete sc (counts as 1 sc-join), 1 more sc in corner, 1 sc in each of next 6 sts of square [*1 sc-join through next st and first empty ch-3 picot at top of next motif, 1 sc in each of next 5 sts, 1 sc-join through next st and next ch-3 picot of same motif, 1 sc in each of next 7 sts. Rep from * 8 times, ending last rep with 1 sc in each of last 6 sts of side, 1 sc in corner st, 1 sc-join through corner st and ch-3 picot of corner motif, 1 more sc in corner, 1 sc in each of first 6 sts of next side]. Rep within brackets twice; then rep from * on last side, ending last rep with 1 sc in each of last 6 sts, 1 sc in corner st. Join to first corner st with sl st. Fasten off.

Border for center square: With *wrong* side facing you, attach yarn in any corner sc of center square. [(1 hdc, 1 sl st, 1 hdc) in corner st, *1 sl st, 1 hdc in next st. Rep from * across side, ending with 1 sl st in last st before corner]. Rep within brackets 3 times. Join to first hdc with sl st. Fasten off.

Border: With front facing you, attach yarn in right-hand bottom ch-3 picot of any corner motif. [(Ch 7, 1 sc in next ch-3 picot of corner motif) twice, ch 7, 1 sc in ch-5 loop. *Ch 7, 1 sc in first ch-3 picot of next motif, ch 5, 1 sc in next ch-3 picot of same motif. Rep from * 8 times, ending side with ch 7, 1 sc in ch-5 loop, ch 7, 1 sc in first ch-3 picot of corner motif]. Rep within brackets 3 times. Join to first ch-3 picot with sl st.

Rnd 2: Ch 4 (counts as 1 tr), 6 tr in first ch-7 loop of corner, ch 5, 7 tr in next ch-7 loop of corner, ch 5, 7 tr in next ch-7 loop, [*(6 tr, ch 2, 6 tr) in next ch-7 loop, 1 sc in next ch-5 loop. Rep from * 8 times, 7 tr in next ch-7 loop, 7 tr in first ch-7 loop of corner, ch 5, 7 tr in next ch-7 loop of corner, 7 tr in next ch-7 loop]. Rep within brackets twice, then rep from * 8 times on last side, 7 tr in last ch-7 loop. Join to top of starting ch-4 with sl st.

Rnd 3: Ch 1, [1 hdc in each of first 7 tr, (3 hdc, ch 5, 3 hdc) in ch-5 corner, (1 hdc in each of next 7 tr) twice, *1 hdc in each of next 6 tr, (1 hdc, ch 3, 1 hdc) in ch-2 sp, 1 hdc in each of next 6 tr; working *over* the next sc and into the ch-5 sp below, work 1 pineapple. Rep from * 7 times, 1 hdc in each of next 6 tr, (1 hdc, ch 3, 1 hdc) in ch-2 sp, 1 hdc in each of next 6 tr, 1 hdc in each of next 7 tr]. Rep within brackets 3 times. Join to first hdc with sl st.

Rnd 4: Work in *back loops only*. Ch 1, (1 sc, ch 2) in each of first 10 hdc, [in ch-5 corner, work (2 sc, ch 5, 2 sc, ch 2), (1 sc, ch 2) in each of next 17 hdc, *(1 sc, ch 2) in each of next 7 hdc; in ch-3 picot, work (1 sc, ch 4, 1 sc, ch 2), (1 sc, ch 2) in each of next 6 hdc, 1 sc in next hdc, 1 sc in pineapple. Rep from * until you have worked in last pineapple of side. Work (1 sc, ch 2) in each of next 17 hdc]. Rep within brackets 3 times, ending last rep with (1 sc, ch 2) in each of last 7 sts. Join to first sc with sl st. Fasten off.

Openwork Squares Afghan

Approximate finished size: Adjustable by multiple of 7 inches plus 6 inches for border; as shown, 48 inches by 62 inches
No experience needed

If you are looking for a design for a large bedspread, this is a good one to consider. Because the motifs are mostly openwork, each motif takes only minutes to make. Yet the solid single-crochet outer rows that border each motif provide the structure and weight appropriate to a bedspread. In this, unlike most openwork, the motifs are joined after they are all completed, a big plus when making a large project. Make sure that you display the spread on a solid background of a contrasting color, or the lively effect of the openwork design will be lost.

Materials:
Unger Utopia, 100-gram skeins:
  10 skeins color 134 (dark teal)
Crochet hook, size H

Gauge: 1 motif = 7 inches on each side

Squares: Make 48. Ch 5; join to first ch with sl st to make a ring.
Rnd 1: Ch 3 (counts as 1 dc), 2 dc in ring, *ch 3, 3 dc in ring. Rep from * twice, ch 3, join to top of ch-3 with sl st.
Rnd 2: Sl st in next dc, *ch 5, 5 dc in next ch-3 sp, ch 5, 1 sc in center dc of next 3-dc group. Rep from * 3 times, working last sc in st holding first sl st. Do not join.
Rnd 3: Sl st into first ch-5 sp, ch 3 (counts as 1 dc), 4 dc in ch-5 sp, *ch 7, 1 sc in center (third) dc of 5-dc group, ch 7, 5 dc in each of next two ch-5 sps. Rep from * 3 times, ending last rep with 5 dc in last ch-5 sp. Join to top of ch-3 with sl st.
Rnd 4: Ch 1, 1 sc in each of first 5 dc, *3 sc in first ch-7 sp, ch 2, 3 sc in next ch-7 sp, 1 sc in each of next 10 dc. Rep from * 3 times, ending last rep with 1 sc in each of last 5 sts. Join to first sc with sl st.
Rnd 5: Ch 1, 1 sc in each of first 8 sts, *3 sc in ch-2 corner, 1 sc in each of next 16 sc. Rep from * 3 times, ending last rep with 1 sc in each of last 8 sc. Join to first sc with sl st.
Rnd 6: Ch 1, 1 sc in each of first 9 sts, *3 sc in corner, 1 sc in each of next 18 sts. Rep from * 3 times, ending last rep with 1 sc in each of last 9 sts. Join to first sc with sl st. Fasten off.

Join motifs: With front sides facing you, join motifs with sl st through all four loops of opposing sts into a rectangle six motifs wide and eight motifs long.

Border: Work 4 rnds of dc around entire joined piece, working 3 dc in corners. Fasten off.

Tassels: Make 4. For each tassel, wrap yarn around a 14-inch piece of stiff cardboard 60 times and cut at one end. Tie a short piece of yarn around the end you did not cut. Tie another short piece of yarn around the doubled strands about 2 inches from the top. Trim the ends evenly. Attach tassels at corners.

Summery Clouds Afghan

Approximate finished size: Adjustable to any multiple of 10 inches; as shown, 50 inches on each side
Average experience needed

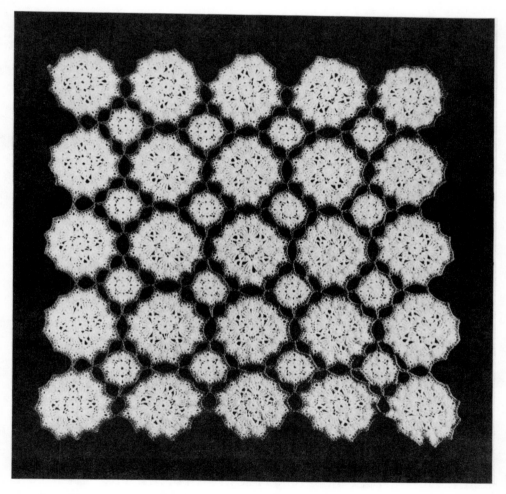

The texture of this diaphanous machine-washable yarn is truly as soft and airy as a cloud. I used white and two delicate shades of blue to paint my summer clouds. Other colors can create different moods. Imagine pale peach shading into mauve for the look of clouds at sunset. Or, for a completely different feeling, use a dark color, perhaps even indigo, for the center rounds and increasingly lighter shades for the two outer rounds. Emphasize the openwork design by displaying the afghan on a background of a contrasting color.

Materials:
Reynolds Kitten, 50-gram skeins:
  5 skeins color 90 (white)
  3 skeins color 19 (light blue)
  2 skeins color 15 (dark blue)
Crochet hook, size I

Gauge: Round 1 = 1½-inch diameter; 1 motif = 10-inch diameter

Note: Instructions for working in one loop only and for working over one row into the row below are given in "Terms and Techniques." Instructions for joining as you work are given in "Finishing Techniques."

Pineapple stitch: In next st, (yo and draw up a loop) 4 times, yo and draw through all but one loop on hook, yo and draw through last two loops on hook.

Motifs: Make 25, joined in 5 rows of 5.
First Motif: With white, ch 4.
Rnd 1: 15 dc in fourth ch from hook—16 dc. Join to top ch of ch-3.
Rnd 2: Work in *back loops only.* Ch 1, 1 sc in first st, *skip next st, (3 dc, ch 1, 3 dc) in next st, skip next st, 1 sc in next st. Rep from * 3 times, ending last rep with sl st in first sc.
Rnd 3: Ch 4 (counts as 1 tr), (3 tr, ch 1, 4 tr) in first sc, *(1 dc, ch 2, 1 dc) in next ch-1 sp, (4 tr, ch 1, 4 tr) in next sc. Rep from * twice, (1 dc, ch 2, 1 dc) in last ch-1 sp. Join to top of starting ch-4 with sl st.
Rnd 4: Work in *back loops only.* 1 sc in each of first 4 tr, *1 sc in ch-1 sp, 1 sc in each of next 4 tr, skip next dc, 3 sc in ch-2 sp, skip next dc, 1 sc in each of next 4 tr. Rep from * 3 times, ending last rep with 3 sc in last ch-2 sp, skip last dc. Join with sl st to first sc.
Rnd 5: Ch 1, 1 sc in first st, *skip next st, 5 dc (1 shell) in next st, skip next st, 1 sc in next st. Rep from * 11 times, ending last rep with skip last st—12 shells. Join to first sc with sl st. Fasten off.
Rnd 6: Attach light blue in center (third) dc of last completed shell. (*Note:* It is important to begin in this shell so that motifs will be correctly aligned when joined.) Work in *back loops only.* Ch 1, 3 sc in center dc of shell, 1 sc in each of next 2 dc; working over the sc of Rnd

5, work 1 pineapple into sc below of Rnd 4, 1 sc in each of next 2 dc. Rep from * 11 times. On last st, change to dark blue and join to first sc with sl st.

Rnd 7: With dark blue, ch 1, 1 sc in first st, *(1 sc, ch 2, 1 sc) in center st of 3-sc group, 1 sc in each of next 2 sc, one 3-sc dec in next sc, pineapple, and first sc of next shell, 1 sc in each of next 2 sts. Rep from * 11 times, ending last rep with 1 sc in last st. Join to first sc with sl st. Fasten off.

Subsequent motifs: When joining motif to one other motif, work Rnd 7 as above but rep from * 9 times (2 shells remain empty) and then work as follows: *1 sc in center st of shell, ch 1, sl st into ch-2 picot of opposing shell of completed motif, ch 1, 1 more sc in center st, 1 sc in each of next 2 sts, one 3-sc dec in next 3 sts, 1 sc in each of next 2 sts. Rep from * once, ending last rep with 1 sc in last st. Join with sl st to first sc. Fasten off.

When joining to two other motifs, work Rnd 7 as above but rep from * 6 times (5 shells remain empty) and then join the next two shells to the opposing shells of the motif at right, work 1 shell without joining, then join the last two shells to the motif above.

Fill: With white, work as for motif through Rnd 2. Fasten off.

Rnd 3: Attach light blue in any ch-1 sp. Ch 1, *3 sc in ch-1 sp; in next sc, work (3 dc, ch 1, 3 dc). Rep from * 3 times. Change to dark blue and join with sl st to first sc.

Rnd 4: With dark blue, ch 1, 1 sc in first st, *1 sc in center dc of 3-dc group, ch 2, sl st around join between motifs, ch 2, 1 more sc in center dc, 1 sc in each of next 4 sts, 1 sc in ch-1 sp, 1 sc through *both* ch-1 sp of shell being joined and ch-2 picot of opposing shell of motif, 1 more sc in ch-1 sp, 1 sc in each of next 4 sts. Rep from * 3 times, ending last rep with 1 sc in each of last 3 sts. Join to first sc with sl st. Fasten off.

Spider's Web Pillow

*Approximate finished size: Adjustable to any multiple of 4½ inches;
as shown, 18 inches on each side*
Average experience needed

Some very lacy openwork designs, such as this one, need to be stretched before their intricate patterns can be clearly seen. Depending on the yarn used, these airy motifs might become a lovely shawl, tablecloth, or window curtain. Each of these would need the weight of heavy fringe or a deep border pattern, such as that used for the Lace Shawl, to pull the design into the stretched shape necessary for it to be fully appreciated.

Materials:
Unger Utopia, 100-gram skeins:
  ¼ skein color 134 (dark teal)
Crochet hook, size I
For pillow:
  Two 18½-inch squares of fabric, color-coordinated with yarn
  Sewing thread to match fabric
  Polyester stuffing

Gauge: 1 motif = 4½-inch diameter

Note: Instructions for joining as you work and making a pillow are given in "Finishing Techniques."

Motifs: Make 16, joined in four rows of four motifs.
First motif: Ch 6, join to first ch with sl st to make ring.
Rnd 1: Ch 1, *(1 sc, 1 hdc, 1 dc, 1 hdc, 1 sc) in ring, ch 9. Rep from * 3 times—4 shells and 4 ch-9 loops. Join to first sc with sl st.
Rnd 2: Sl st into next st, *1 sc in center dc of shell, ch 6; in ch-9 loop, work (1 sc, ch 3, 1 sc, ch 5, 1 sc, ch 3, 1 sc), ch 6. Rep from * 3 times. Join to first sl st with sl st. Fasten off.

Subsequent motifs: When joining to one other motif, work Rnd 2 as above but rep from * *once* and then work as follows: 1 sc in next center dc, ch 6; in ch-9 loop, work (1 sc, ch 3, 1 sc), ch 2, sl st into ch-5 picot of opposing motif, ch 2, sl st into ch-6 loop of opposing motif, ch 2, 1 sc in center dc, ch 2, sl st into next ch-6 loop of opposing motif, ch 2, rep within parentheses, ch 6, join with sl st to first sc. Fasten off.
When joining to two other motifs, work in only one ch-9 loop without joining; then join as above in next three ch-9 loops.

Finishing: Make and stuff an 18-inch pillow and sew the crocheted piece to one side of it.

Lace Shawl

Approximate finished size: 60 inches across top; 40 inches from top to bottom point
Experience needed

This shawl captures the delicate look of old-fashioned lace but eliminates the tedious and time-consuming effort needed to create it. Made with a very large hook and thin cotton yarn, each motif takes only minutes to complete. The shawl is deceiving in another way—its expensive-looking elegance can be created for under six dollars.

Materials:
J. & P. Coats Knit-Cro-Sheen:
  4 balls color 42, cream
Crochet hook, size J

Gauge: 2 rounds = 3-inch diameter; 1 motif = 8-inch diameter

Note: Instructions for working in one loop only are given in "Terms and Techniques." Instructions for joining as you work are given in "Finishing Techniques."

Middle loop: The half-double crochet stitches in this project appear to have three loops: one on the back, one on the front, and one in between at the top of the stitch. This loop, actually the front loop, is the correct one in which to work. For this project, it will be called the "middle loop." When working a round in the middle loop, always join the round with a slip stitch through *both* the middle and back loops.

Double sl-st joins: When you add the side and top fills, you will work 1 sl st in each of two ch-2 spaces of the large motifs. When these are used later for adding the border, they will be called "double sl-st joins."

Pineapple stitch: In next st, (yo and draw up a loop) 4 times, yo and draw through all but one loop on hook, yo and draw through last two loops on hook.

Motifs: Make 16, joining as you work.
First motif: Ch 5, join to first ch with sl st to make ring.
Rnd 1: 12 hdc in ring—12 sts. Join to first hdc with sl st.
Rnd 2: Work in *middle loop only.* Ch 1, (1 hdc, ch 1) in each st—24 sts. Join to first hdc with sl st.
Rnd 3: Ch 1, 2 hdc in every ch-1 sp—24 sts. Join to first hdc with sl st.
Rnd 4: Rep Rnd 2—48 sts; 24 ch-1 sps.
Rnd 5: Rep Rnd 3—48 sts.
Rnd 6: Work in *middle loop only.* Ch 1, 1 hdc in first hdc, *ch 2, skip 1 st, 1 hdc in next st. Rep from * to form 24 ch-2 sps, ending last rep with sl st in first hdc. Fasten off.

Subsequent motifs: Follow the placement diagram for position of motifs. When joining motif to one other motif, work Rnd 6 as above until you have completed 20 ch-2 sps and 7 sts of Rnd 5 remain empty. Ch 1, sl st into ch-2 sp of completed motif, ch 1, skip 1 st, 1 hdc in next st, *ch 1, sl st into next ch-2 sp, ch 1, skip 1 st, 1 hdc in next st. Rep from * twice, skip last st. Join to first hdc with sl st. Fasten off.

When joining motif to two other motifs, work until you have completed 14 ch-2 sps and 19 sts are still empty. Join the next 4 ch-2 sps you make to the motif on the right, ending with 1 hdc—10 sts are still empty. (Ch 2, skip 1 st, 1 hdc in next st) twice, making 2 unjoined ch-2 sps—7 sts are still empty. Join the last 4 ch-2 sps to the motif above the one being completed. Join to first hdc with sl st. Fasten off.

Fills: Make 6, one in each of the circular sps between four motifs. Ch 5 and join to first ch with sl st to make ring.
Rnd 1: Ch 1, 12 hdc in ring—12 sts. Join to first hdc with sl st.
Rnd 2: Work in *middle loop only.* Ch 1, 2 hdc in every st—24 sts. Join to first hdc with sl st.
Rnd 3: Work in *middle loop only.* Ch 1, 1 hdc in first st, *ch 2, skip next st, 1 hdc in next st. Rep from * to make 12 ch-2 sps, ending last rep with sl st in first hdc.
Rnd 4: Ch 1, *sl st into next ch-2 sp of fill, ch 3, sl st into sl-st join between two motifs, ch 3, sl st into same ch-2 sp of fill, (sl st into next ch-2 sp of fill, ch 1, sl st into ch-2 sp of motif, ch 1, sl st into same ch-2 sp of fill) twice. Rep from * 3 times, ending last rep with sl st into first sl st of rnd. Fasten off.

Side fills: Make 6, one for each space on sides of shawl. Follow the instructions for fills until you reach Rnd 4. Begin to join in the right-hand sl-st join between two motifs. Ch 1, *sl st into next ch-2 sp of fill, ch 3, sl st into sl-st join between motifs, ch 3, sl st into same ch-2 sp of fill, (sl st into next ch-2 sp of fill, ch 1, sl st into next ch-2 sp of motif, ch 1, sl st into same ch-2 sp of fill) twice. Rep from * once, sl st into next ch-2 sp of fill, ch 3, sl st into each of next two ch-2 sps of motif (double sl-st join made), ch 3, sl st into same ch-2 sp of fill, (sl st into next ch-2 sp of fill, ch 3, sl st into same ch-2 sp of fill) twice making two empty ch-2 sps. Ch 3, sl st into fourth ch-2 sp from sl-st join of next motif, sl st into third ch-2 sp of same motif (double sl-st join made), ch 3, sl st into same ch-2 sp of fill, (sl st into next ch-2 sp of fill, ch 1, sl st into next ch-2 sp of motif, ch 1, sl st into same ch-2 sp of fill) twice. Join to first sl st with sl st. Fasten off.

Top fills: Make 6, one between each two motifs of the top row. These fills are not worked in rnds, but back and forth in rows. Ch 5 and join to first ch with sl st to make ring.

Row 1: Ch 1, 8 hdc in ring. Do not join. Ch 1, turn.

Row 2: Work in *middle loop only.* Work 2 hdc in each st—16 sts. Ch 1, turn.

Row 3: 1 hdc in first st, *ch 2, skip 1 st, 1 hdc in next st. Rep from * 5 times—7 ch-2 sps. Ch 2, turn.

Row 4: Sl st into fourth ch-2 sp from sl-st join of right-hand motif, sl st into third ch-2 sp, ch 2, sl st into first ch-2 sp of fill, (sl st into next ch-2 sp of fill, ch 1, sl st into next ch-2 sp of motif, ch 1, sl st into same ch-2 sp of fill) twice, sl st into last ch-2 sp of fill, ch 2, sl st into each of next two ch-2 sps of motif, ch 2, sl st into same ch-2 sp of fill. Fasten off.

Top bar: With wrong side facing you, attach yarn in the fifth ch-2 sp to the right of the first double sl-st join of the first top fill. Ch 6 (counts as 1 tr, ch 2), (1 tr in next ch-2 sp, ch 2) 4 times, *1 tr in double sl-st join, ch 8, 1 sc in center ch-5 ring of fill, ch 8, 1 tr in next double sl-st join, (ch 2, 1 tr in next sp) twice, ch 2. Rep from * 5 times, ending last rep with (ch 2, 1 tr in next ch-2 sp) 5 times. Ch 1, turn.

Row 2: 3 sc in each of first five ch-2 sps, *8 sc in ch-8 loop, 1 sc in next sc, 8 sc in next ch-8 loop, (3 sc in next ch-2 sp) 3 times. Rep from * across top, ending last rep with 3 sc in each of last five ch-2 sps. Fasten off.

Border: With front facing you, attach yarn in side of last sc of top bar.

Row 1: Ch 4 (counts as 1 sc, ch 3), 1 sc in side of tr, ch 3, 1 sc in base of tr, (1 sc in next ch-2 sp, ch 3) 9 times, *1 dc in double sl-st join, ch 3, (1 dc in next ch-2 sp of fill, ch 3) 4 times, 1 dc in next double sl-st join, ch 3, (1 sc in next ch-2 sp of motif, ch 3) 8 times. Rep from * until you reach bottom motif, (1 sc in next ch-2 sp, ch 3) 6 times; in next (bottom) ch-2 sp, work (1 sc, ch 3, 1 sc, ch 3), (1 sc in next ch-2 sp, ch 3) 6 times. Rep from * to top motif, ending with (1 sc in next ch-2 sp, ch 3) 9 times, 1 sc in base of tr, ch 3, 1 sc in side of tr, ch 3, 1 sc in side of sc of top bar. Ch 1, turn. (*Note:* The ch-3 sp between the 2 sc in the bottom is the ch-3 corner.)

Row 2: Work 4 sc in every ch-3 sp to corner, 9 sc in corner, 4 sc in every ch-3 sp to top, ending with sl st into sc of top bar. Ch 2, turn. (Fifth st of 9-st corner group is corner st.)

Row 3: Work in *back loops only.* 1 pineapple in first st, *ch 2, skip 1 st, 1 pineapple in next st. Rep from * until 1 st remains before corner st, ch 2, skip last st, (1 pineapple, ch 2, 1 pineapple) in corner st. Rep from * to top. Ch 2, turn.

Row 4: Work 2 dc in every ch-2 sp to corner ch-2, 5 dc in corner, 2 dc in every ch-2 sp to top. Ch 1, turn.

Row 5: 1 sc in first st, *skip 3 sts, 7 tr (counts as tr shell) in next st, skip 3 sts, 1 sc in next st. Rep from *, ending side with 1 sc in first st of 5-dc corner group, skip next st, 5 tr in corner st, skip next st, 1 sc in last st of 5-dc group. Rep from * to top. Ch 1, turn.

Row 6: 1 sc in first st, *(1 sc, ch 1) in each of first 3 sts of shell, (1 sc, ch 3, 1 sc) in center st of shell, (ch 1, 1 sc) in each of next 3 sts of shell, 1 sc in next sc. Rep from * around border. Fasten off.

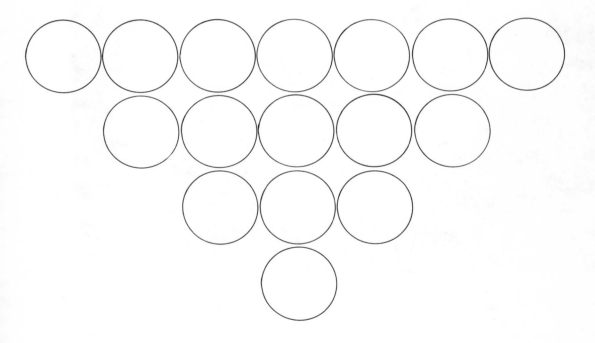

Lace Shawl
Motif-Placement Diagram

Valentine Doily

Approximate finished size: 14-inch heart shape; 4 inches for border
Experience needed

A piece of lace in the tradition of the great early crochet-lacemakers, this project takes skill and concentration. Yet, as is true of any serious art or craft, effort and enterprise are rewarded by the creation of a very special result. Earlier generations would have put this elegant piece of lace on a table or the back of a chair. Instead, why not sew it to a piece of contrasting fabric—velvet, perhaps—mount, and frame it. If you wish, a ribbon may be threaded through the spaces formed by the trebles of the inner edging and then tied at the bottom.

Materials:
Phildar 325 Perle 8, 40-gram balls:
   2 balls color 32, ecru
Crochet hook, size 6 steel
Sewing needle
One sheet graph paper at least 16 inches square, with 8 squares to the
   inch, or photocopy enlargement of heart pattern (see instructions
   under "Finishing").
French curve for shaping paper pattern (optional)

Note: Instructions for the single-crochet post stitch and for working in
one loop only are given in "Terms and Techniques." Instructions for
joining as you work are given in "Finishing Techniques." The heart
must be blocked on a paper pattern to give it the correct size and
shape. As it is being made, it resembles an elongated *V*.

Sl st into ch-5 loop: When the instructions read "sl st into ch-5 loop,"
always work into the third ch of that loop, *not* into the ch-5 loop. In
order to simplify the instructions, the third ch has not been specified
each time.

Shell loops: The shell loops are the two ch-5 loops over the 9-dc shells.
They are not used when joining the large motifs; only the four ch-5
loops between the shell loops are used. The shell loops are used to join
the fills.

Double treble: Yo three times, insert hook in stitch and draw up a
loop, (yo and draw through two loops) 4 times.

Motifs: Make 12, joining as you work. Follow the placement diagram
for position of motifs and order of joining.
First motif: Ch 8, join to first ch with sl st to make ring.
Rnd 1: Ch 1, 24 sc in ring—24 sts. Join to first sc with sl st.
Rnd 2: Ch 1, 1 sc in first st, *ch 4, skip next 3 sts, 1 sc in next st. Rep
from * 5 times, ending last rep with sl st in first sc—six ch-4 loops.
Rnd 3: In each ch-4 loop, work (1 sl st, ch 2, 8 dc, ch 2, 1 sl st)—6
petals.

Rnd 4: Ch 1, 1 sc post st around post of first sc of Rnd 2, *ch 4, 1 sc post st around post of next sc of Rnd 2. Rep from * 5 times, ending last rep with sl st in first sc—six ch-4 loops.

Rnd 5: In each ch-4 loop, work (1 sl st, ch 2, 6 dc, ch 2, 1 sl st)—6 petals.

Rnd 6: Sl st up side of first petal to first dc. Ch 1, *1 sc in first dc of petal, ch 5, skip 4 sts, 1 sc in last dc of petal, ch 5. Rep from * 5 times—12 ch-5 loops. Join with sl st to first sc.

Rnd 7: Sl st in each of first 2 chs, *sl st in ch-5 loop, ch 5. Rep from * 11 times—12 ch-5 loops. Join to sl st, holding first ch-5 with sl st.

Rnd 8: Sl st into first ch-5 loop. Ch 3 (counts as 1 dc), 8 dc in ch-5 loop, *(ch 5, sl st into next ch-5 loop) twice, ch 5, 9 dc (counts as 1 shell) in next ch-5 loop. Rep from * twice, (ch 5, sl st into next ch-5 loop) twice, ch 5—4 shells. Join with sl st to top ch of ch-3.

Rnd 9: *Ch 5, sl st to center (fifth) dc of shell, ch 5, sl st in last dc of shell, (ch 5, sl st into next ch-5 loop) 3 times, ch 5, sl st in first dc of next shell. Rep from * 3 times—24 ch-5 loops. Fasten off.

Subsequent motifs: When joining a motif to one other motif, work until you have completed the third rep of Rnd 9 and there are three ch-5 loops of Rnd 8 still empty. Ch 2, sl st into first ch-5 loop of opposing motif, *ch 2, sl st into next ch-5 loop of motif being joined, ch 2, sl st into next ch-5 loop of completed motif. Rep from * twice, ch 2, sl st into first sl st of rnd. Fasten off.

When joining a motif to two other motifs, work until you have completed the two ch-5 loops over the second shell. Join the next set of loops to be made to the opposing set of loops on the right-hand motif, ending with ch 2, 1 sl st in first dc of next shell. Ch 5, sl st in first dc of shell, ch 5, sl st in center dc of shell, ch 5, sl st in last dc of shell. Join last set of loops to be made to the left-hand completed motif.

Floral fills: Make 5, one in each circular sp between four motifs. Follow the instructions for motifs until you have completed Rnd 5.

Rnd 6: Sl st up side of first petal, *sl st in first dc of petal, ch 2, sl st into first shell loop of motif, ch 2, sl st in last dc of petal, ch 2, sl st into next shell loop of motif, ch 2, sl st in first st of next petal, ch 3, sl st into sl-st join between motifs, ch 3, sl st in last dc of petal. Rep from * 3 times, ending last rep with sl st in first sl st of rnd. Fasten off.

Top floral fills: Join as for floral fills, but rep from * once. Then continue to work as you did for Rnd 6 of motifs, ending with 1 sl st in last dc of last petal, ch 2, sl st into ch-5 loop of first motif to the *right* of the first shell loops used, ch 2, sl st into first petal of fill. Fasten off.

Join the center of the heart: To pull the heart together at the center, motifs 9, 8, and 11 must be joined. Attach yarn in the third ch of the first ch-5 loop to the left of the shell loops at the top of motif 9. *Ch 2, sl st into opposing ch-5 loop of motif 11, ch 2, sl st into next ch-5 loop of motif 9. Rep from * to join each opposing pair of loops, including shell loops, of the two motifs, ending with ch 2, sl st into last loop of motif 11. Ch 2, sl st into sl-st join between motifs 11 and 8, ch 2, sl st into first shell loop of motif 8, ch 2, sl st into sl-st join between motifs 9 and 11, ch 2, sl st into next shell loop of motif 8, ch 2, sl st into sl-st join between motifs 8 and 9, ch 2, sl st into sl-st join between motifs 9 and 11. Fasten off.

Center chain mesh fill: With the front facing you, attach yarn in first loop to the right of (above) the shell loops on the side of motif 10.
Row 1: Ch 5, sl st in first shell loop of motif 10, ch 5, sl st in next shell loop, 7 dc in sl-st join between motifs 10 and 9, sl st in first shell loop of motif 9, ch 5, sl st in next shell loop, ch 5, sl st in next ch-5 loop, 7 dc in sl-st join between motifs 9 and 11, sl st in next ch-5 loop, ch 5, sl st in first shell loop of motif 11, ch 5, sl st in next shell loop, 7 dc in sl-st join between motifs 11 and 12, sl st in first shell loop of motif 12, ch 5, sl st in next shell loop, ch 5, sl st in next ch-5 loop. Ch 1, turn.
Row 2: Sl st to third ch of ch-5 loop just completed. Ch 5, sl st in next ch-5 loop, ch 5, sl st in center (fourth) dc of shell, *(ch 5, sl st in next ch-5 loop) twice, ch 5, sl st in center dc of next shell. Rep from * once, (ch 5, sl st in next loop) twice. Ch 1, turn.
Row 3: Sl st to third ch of loop just completed, (ch 5, sl st into next ch-5 loop) 9 times. Ch 1, turn.
Row 4: Sl st to third ch of ch-5 loop just completed, (ch 5, sl st in next ch-5 loop) 3 times, (ch 2, sl st in next ch-5 loop) twice, (ch 5, sl st in next ch-5 loop) 3 times. Fasten off.

Top inner chain mesh fill: Right fill is worked between top floral fill and motif 10; left fill is worked between top floral fill and motif 12.
Right fill: With *wrong* side facing you, attach yarn in the first loop to the *right* of the shell loops at top of motif 10.
Row 1: (Ch 5, sl st in next ch-5 loop) twice, ch 5, sl st in sl-st join between motif 10 and fill, ch 5, sl st in first ch-5 loop of fill. Ch 1, turn.
Row 2: Sl st to third ch of ch-5 loop just completed, (ch 5, sl st in next ch-5 loop) 3 times. Fasten off.
Left fill: Work as for right fill but begin with *front* side facing you.

Top outer chain mesh fill: Right fill is worked between top floral fill and motif 4; left fill is worked between top floral fill and motif 7.

Right fill: With front facing you, attach yarn in first ch-5 loop to the left of (above) the shell loops on the side of motif 4. (Ch 5, sl st in next loop) twice, ch 5, sl st in sl-st join between motif and fill, ch 5, sl st in first ch-5 loop of fill. Ch 1, turn.

Row 2: Sl st to third ch of ch-5 loop just completed, (ch 5, sl st in next loop) twice. Fasten off.

Left fill: Work as above, but begin with the *wrong* side facing you.

Side chain mesh fills: Make 6, one in each sp between two motifs on the sides.

Right side: With front side facing you, attach yarn in the ch-5 loop to the *right* of the top shell loops of the lower motif.

Row 1: Ch 5, sl st into first shell loop of lower motif, ch 5, sl st into next shell loop, 7 dc in sl-st join between motifs, sl st in first shell loop of top motif, ch 5, sl st in next shell loop, ch 5, sl st in next ch-5 loop. Ch 1, turn.

Row 2: Sl st to third ch of ch-5 loop just completed, ch 5, sl st in next ch-5 loop, ch 5, sl st in center dc of shell, (ch 5, sl st in next ch-5 loop) twice. Ch 1, turn.

Row 3: Sl st to third ch of ch-5 loop just completed. Ch 3, sl st in next ch-5 loop, ch 5, sl st in next ch-5 loop, ch 3, sl st in next ch-5 loop. Fasten off.

Left side: Work as above but attach yarn in upper rather than lower motif.

Bottom point: With front facing you, attach yarn in first shell loop at bottom of motif 1, ch 5, sl st into next shell loop. Fasten off.

Border: The border is made separately, then sewn to the heart.

Base scallop: Ch 8, join to first ch with sl st to make a ring.

Row 1: Ch 3 (counts as 1 dc), 16 dc in ring—17 sts. Turn.

Row 2: Work in *loops closest to you only.* Ch 4 (counts as 1 dc, ch 1), (1 dc, ch 1) in each dc—16 ch-1 sps. Turn.

Row 3: Ch 5 (counts as 1 dc, ch 2), *1 dc in next dc, ch 2. Rep from * 14 times, 1 dc in third ch of ch-4—16 ch-2 sps. Turn.

Row 4: Ch 6 (counts as 1 dc, ch 3), *1 dc in next dc, ch 3. Rep from * 14 times, 1 dc in third ch of ch-5—16 ch-3 sps. Turn.

Row 5: Ch 7 (counts as 1 dc, ch 4), *1 dc in next dc, ch 4. Rep from * 14 times, 1 dc in third ch of ch-6—16 ch-4 sps.

Row 6: Ch 8 (counts as 1 dc, ch 5), *1 dc in next dc, ch 5. Rep from * 14 times, 1 dc in third ch of ch-7—16 ch-5 sps. Ch 1, turn.

Row 7: In each ch-5 sp, work (1 sc, 5 dc, 1 sc)—16 shells. *Turn.*

Begin next scallop: Ch 8, sl st in center dc of last completed shell of base scallop. Ch 1, turn.

Row 1: Sl st into ch-8 ring, ch 3 (counts as 1 dc), 8 dc in ring—9 dc. Turn.

Row 2: Rep Row 2 of base scallop to make 8 ch-1 sps, ending with sl st into center dc of next shell of base. Turn.

Row 3: Rep Row 3 of base scallop.

Row 4: Rep Row 4 of base scallop, ending with sl st in center dc of next shell of base. Turn.

Row 5: Rep Row 5 of base scallop.

Row 6: Rep Row 6 of base scallop, ending with sl st in center dc of next shell. Turn.

Row 7: Rep Row 7 of base scallop. Turn.

Subsequent scallops: Rep the instructions for the 8 ch-sp scallop 7 more times. After you have completed the eighth small scallop, *do not* fasten off but pull up a long loop so that the side won't unravel. After you have completed the second strip of scallops, you will make one more scallop on this row, joining the two strips.

Begin a new strip of scallops: Ch 8, join to first ch with sl st to make a ring.

Row 1: Ch 3 (counts as 1 dc), 8 dc in ring—9 dc. Turn.

Rows 2 through 7: Rep Rows 2 through 7 of base, but to make 8 ch-sps. Rep the instructions for 8 ch-sp scallops until you have completed eight scallops, *not* including the first you made. At the end of the eighth scallop, *do not turn.* The next scallop will be joined to both the one before it, as you have been doing, and to the first eight shells of the empty side of the base scallop. When you have completed this scallop, there should be eight shells left empty at the bottom of the base scallop.

Joining scallop: With the fronts of both strips facing you, ch 4, sl st into the first st of the first shell of the base scallop and into each of the next 3 sts of that shell until you reach the center st. Ch 4, sl st into the center st of the first shell of the eighth scallop. Ch 1, turn.

Row 1: Ch 3 (counts as 1 dc), 8 dc in ch-4 sp, ch 3 (counts as first dc of next row), sl st in center st of second shell of base. Turn.

Row 2: Ch 1 (counts as ch-1 sp), rep rest of Row 2, ending with sl st into next shell of eighth scallop. Turn.

Row 3: Rep Row 3, ending with ch-3 (counts as first dc of next row), sl st in next shell of base. Turn.

Row 4: Ch 3 (counts as first ch-3 sp) rep rest of Row 4, ending with sl st into center of next shell of eighth scallop. Turn.

Row 5: Rep Row 5, ending with ch-3 (counts as first dc of next row), sl st in next shell of base. Turn.

Row 6: Ch 5 (counts as first ch-5 sp), rep rest of Row 6, ending with sl st into next shell of eighth scallop. Turn.

Row 7: Rep Row 7, ending with sl st in same shell of base scallop as used in Row 5. Fasten off.

Top joining scallop: Complete the border by working the ninth scallop of the first strip just as you worked the scallop joining the second strip and the base, but between the eighth scallop of the first strip and the four empty shells of the first scallop of the second strip. At the end of Row 7, fasten off.

Inner edging of border: This row is worked around the inside edge of the border. As you work, don't work into the sides of the dcs, but around the posts into the ch-sps. Attach yarn in ch-8 ring of base scallop. Ch 4 (counts as 1 tr), 2 tr in ch-8 ring, ch 2, skip Row 1 of base scallop, 2 tr in Row 3, *ch 2, skip next row, 2 tr in next row. Rep from * around piece to ch-8 ring of top base scallop. In ch-8 ring, work (2 tr, ch 2) twice, 1 tr, 1 dtr, 1 tr, (ch 2, 2 tr) twice. *Ch 2, skip next row, 2 tr in next row. Rep from * around piece to base, ending with 2 tr in Row 2 of base, skip Row 1. Join to top of ch-4 with sl st. Fasten off.

Finishing: Make a paper pattern, following the graph pattern given. A French curve—a clear plastic, irregular curve used in dressmaking—is useful but not necessary to produce a smooth, even curve. If you prefer, have your local copy center enlarge the pattern so that 8 squares of the grid = 1 inch. Put the paper pattern on your blocking board and pin the heart to it to produce the heart shape before you block. With wrong sides facing you and using a sewing needle, sew the trim to the heart. Pin the heart back to the pattern with the border outside the edge of the pattern and reblock.

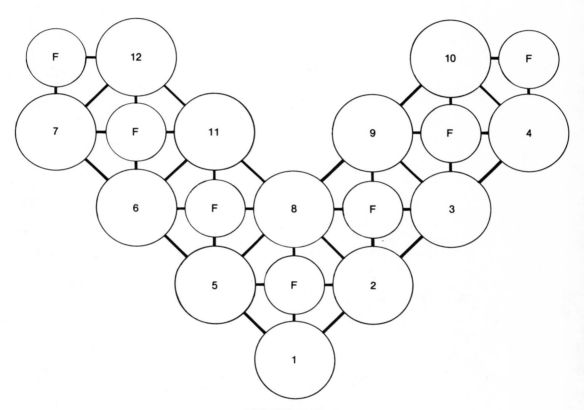

Valentine Doily
Motif-Placement Diagram

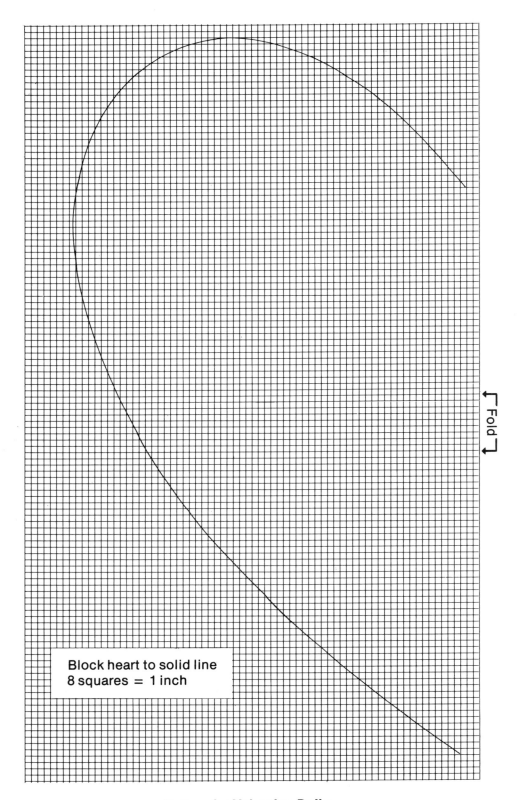

Fold

Block heart to solid line
8 squares = 1 inch

Pattern for Valentine Doily

Yarn Buying Guide

All the yarns used in this book are nationally available. If you cannot find a particular yarn, write to the appropriate yarn company for information on mail-order buying and/or availability in your area.

Bernat Yarn and Craft Corporation
Depot and Mendon Streets, P.O. Box 387
Uxbridge, MA 01569

Brunswick Yarns
Pickens, SC 29671

Coats and Clark Sales Corp.
72 Cummings Point Road
Stamford, CT 06902

Laines Anny Blatt
24770 Crestview Court
Farmington Hills, MI 48018

Lily Craft Products
140 Kero Road
Carlstadt, NJ 07072

Phildar Incorporated
6438 Dawson Boulevard
Norcross, GA 30093

Reynolds Yarns, Inc.
15 Oser Avenue
Hauppage, NY 11788

William Unger & Co., Inc.
P.O. Box 1621
Bridgeport, CT 06601

Index